Y0-CVI-100

*"TOLD
THROUGH
THE
AGES"*

HEROES OF MODERN EUROPE

TOLD THROUGH THE AGES

Legends of Greece and Rome
Favourite Greek Myths
Stories of Robin Hood and his Merry Outlaws
Stories of King Arthur and his Knights
Stories from Herodotus
Stories from Wagner
Britain Long Ago
Stories from Scottish History
Stories from Greek Tragedy
Stories from Dickens
Stories from the Earthly Paradise
Stories from the Æneid
The Book of Rustem
Stories from Chaucer
Stories from the Old Testament
Stories from the Odyssey
Stories from the Iliad
Told by the Northmen
Stories from Don Quixote
The Story of Roland
Stories from Thucydides
The Story of Hereward
Stories from the Faerie Queene
Cuchulain: The Hound of Ulster
Stories from Xenophon
Old Greek Nature Stories
Stories from Shakespeare
Stories from Dante
Famous Voyages of the Great Discoverers
The Story of Napoleon
Stories of Pendennis and the Charterhouse
Sir Guy of Warwick
Heroes of the Middle Ages
The Story of the Crusades
The Story of Nelson
Stories from George Eliot
The Boys' Froissart
Shakespeare's Stories of the English Kings
Heroes of Modern Europe
The Story of King Robert the Bruce
Stories of the Scottish Border
The Story of the French Revolution
The Story of Wellington
The Story of Lord Roberts
The Story of Lord Kitchener
Stories of the Saints
The Story of St Elizabeth of Hungary
In Feudal Times
The High Deeds of Finn
The Story of Early English Travel and Discovery
Legends of Ancient Egypt
The Story of the Renaissance
Boyhood Stories of Famous Men

Other volumes in active preparation

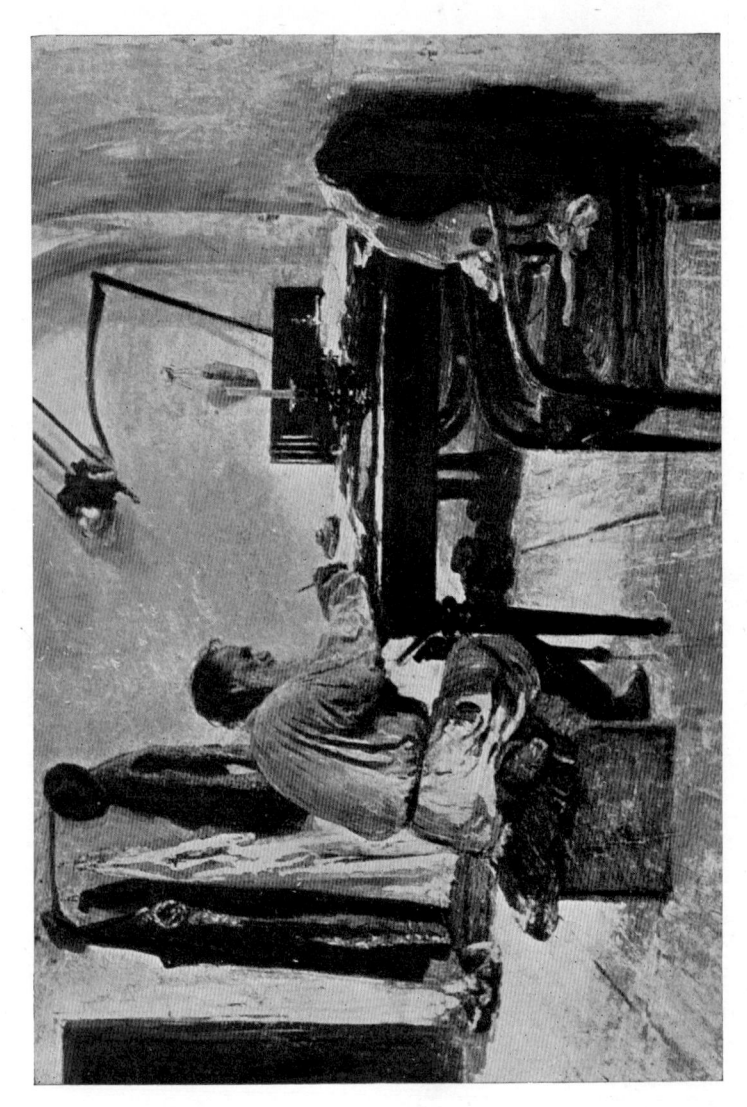

Leo Tolstoy in his bare Apartments at Yasnaya Polyana
Repin

HEROES OF MODERN EUROPE

BY

ALICE BIRKHEAD B.A.

AUTHOR OF
'THE STORY OF THE FRENCH REVOLUTION'
'MARIE ANTOINETTE' 'PETER THE GREAT' ETC.

WITH EIGHT ILLUSTRATIONS

GEORGE G. HARRAP & CO. LTD.
LONDON   CALCUTTA   SYDNEY

*First published July 1913
by* GEORGE G. HARRAP *& Co.
39-41 Parker Street, Kingsway, London, W.C.2
Reprinted in the present series:
February 1914; August 1917; May 1921; January 1924*

Printed in Great Britain by Turnbull & Spears, Edinburgh

Contents

CHAP.		PAGE
I.	THE TWO SWORDS	9
II.	DANTE, THE DIVINE POET	19
III.	LORENZO THE MAGNIFICENT	30
IV.	THE PRIOR OF SAN MARCO	41
V.	MARTIN LUTHER, REFORMER OF THE CHURCH	52
VI.	CHARLES V, HOLY ROMAN EMPEROR	63
VII.	THE BEGGARS OF THE SEA	74
VIII.	WILLIAM THE SILENT, FATHER OF HIS COUNTRY	86
IX.	HENRY OF NAVARRE	100
X.	UNDER THE RED ROBE	115
XI.	THE GRAND MONARCH	128
XII.	PETER THE GREAT	137
XIII.	THE ROYAL ROBBER	145
XIV.	SPIRITS OF THE AGE	156
XV.	THE MAN FROM CORSICA	163
XVI.	"GOD AND THE PEOPLE"	183
XVII.	"FOR ITALY AND VICTOR EMMANUEL!"	195
XVIII.	THE THIRD NAPOLEON	207
XIX.	THE REFORMER OF THE EAST	216
XX.	THE HERO IN HISTORY	228
	INDEX	233

Illustrations

	PAGE
LEO TOLSTOY IN HIS BARE APARTMENTS AT YASNAYA POLYANA (*Repin*) . . . . . . *Frontispiece*	
DANTE IN THE STREETS OF FLORENCE (*Evelyn Paul*) . .	22
THE LAST SLEEP OF SAVONAROLA (*Sir George Reid, P.R.S.A.*) .	50
PHILIP II PRESENT AT AN AUTO-DA-FÉ (*D. Valdivieso*) . .	76
LAST MOMENTS OF COUNT EGMONT (*Louis Gallait*) . .	90
AN APPLICATION TO THE CARDINAL FOR HIS FAVOUR (*Walter Gay*)	124
FREDERICK THE GREAT RECEIVING HIS PEOPLE'S HOMAGE (*A. Menzel*)	152
THE MEETING OF VICTOR EMMANUEL AND GARIBALDI (*Pietro Aldi*)	204

Heroes of Modern Europe

Chapter I

The Two Swords

IN the fourth century after Christ began that decay of the Roman Empire which had been the pride of the then civilized world. Warriors of Teutonic race invaded its splendid cities, destroyed without remorse the costliest and most beautiful of its antique treasures. Temples and images of the gods fell before barbarians whose only fear was lest they should die " upon the straw," while marble fountains and luxurious bath-houses were despoiled as signs of a most inglorious state of civilization. Theatres perished and, with them, the plays of Greek dramatists, who have found no true successors. Pictures and statues and buildings were defaced where they were not utterly destroyed. The Latin race survived, forlornly conscious of its vanished culture.

The Teutons had hardly begun to impose upon the Empire the rude customs of their own race when Saracens, bent upon spreading the religion of Mahomet, bore down upon Italy, where resistance from watch-towers and castles was powerless to check their cruel depredations. Norman pirates plundered the shores of the Mediterranean and sailed up the River Seine, always winning easy victories. Magyars, a strange, wandering race, came from the East and wrought much evil among the newly-settled Germans.

From the third to the tenth century there were incredible changes among the European nations. Gone were the gleaming cities of the South and the worship of art and science and the exquisite refinements of the life of scholarly leisure. Gone were the flourishing manufactures since the warrior had no time to devote to trading. Gone was the love of letters and the philosopher's prestige now that men looked to the battle-field alone to give them the awards of glory.

Outwardly, Europe of the Middle Ages presented a sad contrast to the magnificence of an Empire which was fading to remoteness year by year. The ugly towns did not attempt to hide their squalor, when dirt was such a natural condition of life that a knight would dwell boastfully upon his contempt for cleanliness, and a beauty display hands innocent of all proper tending. The dress of the people was ill-made and scanty, lacking the severe grace of the Roman toga. Furniture was rudely hewn from wood and placed on floors which were generally uneven and covered with straw instead of being paved with tessellated marble.

Yet the inward life of Europe was purer since it sought to follow the teaching of Christ, and preached universal love and a toleration that placed on the same level a mighty ruler and the lowest in his realm. Fierce spirits, unfortunately, sometimes forgot the truth and gave themselves up to a cruel lust for persecution which was at variance with their creed, but the holiest now condemned warfare and praised the virtues of obedience and self-sacrifice.

The Two Swords

Whereas pagan Greek and Rome had searched for beauty upon earth, it was the dreary belief of the Middle Ages that the world was a place where only misery could be the portion of mankind, who were bidden to look to another life for happiness and pleasure. Sinners hurried from temptation into monasteries, which were founded for the purpose of enabling men to prepare for eternity. Family life was broken up and all the pleasant intercourse of social habits. Marriage was a snare, and even the love of parents might prove dangerous to the devoted monk. Strange was the isolation of the hermit who refused to cleanse himself or change his clothes, desiring above all other things to attain to that blessed state when his soul should be oblivious of his body.

Women also despised the claims of kindred and retired to convents where the elect were granted visions after long prayer and fasting. The nun knelt on the bare stone floor of her cell, awaiting the ecstasy that would descend on her. When it had gone again she was nigh to death, faint and weary, yet compelled to struggle onward till her earthly life came to an end.

The Crusades, or Wars of the Cross, had roused Europe from a state of most distressful bondage. Ignorance and barbarism were shot with gleams of spiritual light even after the vast armies were sent forth to wrest the possession of Jerusalem from the infidels. Shameful stories of the treatment of pilgrims to the Holy Sepulchre had moved the hearts of kings and princes to a passionate indignation. Valour became the highest, and all men were eager to be ranked with Crusaders —those soldiers of heroic courage whose cause was Christianity and its defence. At the close of the tenth century there were innumerable pilgrims travelling toward the Holy Land, for it had been prophesied that in the year A.D. 1000 the end of the world would come, when it would be well for those within Jerusalem, the City of the Saviour. The inhuman conduct of the Turk was resented violently, because it would keep many a sinner from salvation; and the dangerous journey to the East was held to atone for the gravest crimes.

After the first disasters in which so many Crusaders fell before they reached their destination, Italy especially began to benefit by these wars. It was considered safer to reach Jerusalem by sea, boarding the vessels in Italian ports, which were owned and equipped by Italian merchants. Venice, Pisa, and Genoa gradually assumed the trade of ancient Constantinople, once without rival on the southern sea. Constantinople was a city of wonder to the ignorant fighting men from other lands, who had never dreamed of a civilization so complete as that which she possessed. Awed by elegance and luxury, they returned to their homes with a sense of inferiority. They had met and fought side by side with warriors of such polished manners that they felt ashamed of their own brutal ways. They had seen strange costumes and listened to strange tongues. Henceforth no nation of Europe could be entirely indifferent to the fact that there was a world without.

The widowed and desolate were not comforted by the knowledge which the returned Crusader delighted to impart. They had been sacrificed to the pride which led husbands and fathers to sell their estates and squander vast sums of money, that they might equip a band of followers to lead in triumph to the Holy Wars. The complaints of starving women led to the collection of much gold and silver by Lambert Le Bègue, "the stammering priest." He built a number of small houses to be inhabited by the Order of Bèguines, a new sisterhood who did not sever themselves entirely from the world, but lived in peaceful retirement, occupied by spinning and weaving all day long.

The Beghards, or Weaving Brothers, took pattern by this busy guild of workers and followed the same rules of simple piety. They were fond of religious discussion, and were mystics. They enjoyed the approval of Rome until the new orders were established of Saint Francis and Saint Dominic.

In the twelfth century religion was drawing nearer to humanity and the needs of earth. The new orders, therefore, tried to bridge the gulf between the erring and the saintly, forbidding their brethren to seclude themselves from other men. A healthy reaction was taking place from the old idea that the religious life meant a withdrawal from the temptations of the world.

St Dominic, born in Spain in 1170, was the founder of "the Order of Preaching Monks for the conversion of heretics." The first aim of the "Domini canes" (Dominicans), or Hounds of the Lord, was to attack anyone who denied their faith. Cruelty could be practised under the rule of Dominic, who bade his followers lead men by any path to their ultimate salvation. Tolerance of free thought and progress was discouraged, and rigid discipline corrected any disciple of compassion. The dress of the order was severely plain, consisting of a long black mantle over a white robe. The brethren practised poverty, and fared humbly on bread and water.

The brown frocked Franciscans, rivals in later times of the monks of Dominic, were always taught to love mankind and be merciful to transgressors. It was the duty of the Preaching Brothers to warn and threaten; it was the joy of the *Frati Minori*, or Lesser Brothers, to tend the sick and protect the helpless, taking thought for the very birds and fishes.

St Francis was born at Assisi in 1182, the son of a prosperous householder and cloth merchant. He drank and was merry, like any other youth of the period, till a serious illness purged him of follies. After dedicating his life to God, he put down in the market-place of Assisi all he possessed save the shirt on his body. The bitter reproaches of kinsfolk pursued him vainly as he set out in beggarly state to give service to the poor and despised. He loved Nature and her creatures, speaking of the birds as "noble" and holding close communion with them. The saintly Italian was opposed to the warlike doctrines of St Dominic; he made peace very frequently between the two parties known as Guelfs and Ghibellines.

Welf was a common name among the dukes of Bavaria, and the Guelfs were, in general, supporters of the Papacy and this ducal house, whereas the Waiblingen (Ghibellines) received their name from a castle in Swabia, a fief of the Hohenstaufen enemies of the Pope. It was under a famous emperor of the House of Swabia that the struggle between Papacy and Empire, "the two swords," gained attention from the rest of Europe.

In the eleventh century, Pope Gregory VII had won many notable victories in support of his claims to temporal power. He had brought Henry IV, the proud Emperor, before whose name men trembled, to sue for his pardon at Canossa, and had kept the suppliant in the snow, with bare head and bare feet, that he might endure the last humiliations. Then the fortune of war changed, and the Pope was seized in the Church of St Peter at Rome by Cencio, a fiery noble, who held him in close confinement. It was easier to lord it over princes who were hated by many of their own subjects than to quell the animosity which was roused by attempted domination in the Eternal City.

The Pope was able sometimes to elect a partisan of the Guelf party as emperor. On the other hand, an emperor had been heard to lament the election of a staunch friend to the Papacy because he believed that no pope could ever be a true Ghibelline.

Certain princes of the House of Hohenstaufen were too proud to acknowledge an authority that threatened to crush their power in Italy. Henry VI was a ruler dreaded by contemporaries as merciless to the last degree. He burned men alive if they offended him, and had no compunction in ordering the guilty to be tarred and blinded. He was of such a temper that the Pope had not the courage to demand from him the homage of a vassal. It was Frederick II, Henry's son, who came into conflict with the Papacy so violently that all his neighbours watched in terror.

Pope Gregory IX would give no quarter, and excommunicated the Emperor because he had been unable to go on a crusade owing to pestilence in his army. The clergy were bidden to assemble in the Church of St Peter and to fling down their lighted candles as the Pope cursed the Emperor for his broken promise, a sin against religion. The news of this ceremony spread through the world, the two parties appealing to the princes of Europe for aid in fighting out this quarrel. Frederick defied the papal decree, and went to win back Jerusalem from the infidels as soon as his soldiers had recovered. He took the city, but had to crown himself as king since none other would perform the service for a man outside the Church. Frederick bade the pious Mussulmans continue the prayers they would have ceased through deference to a Christian ruler. He had thrown off all the superstitions of the age except the study of astrology, and was a scholar of wide repute, delighting in correspondence with the learned.

The Arabs did not admire Frederick's person, describing him as unlikely to fetch a high price if he had been a slave! He was bald-headed and had weak eyesight, though generally held graceful and attractive. In mental powers he surpassed the greatest of his house, which had always been famous for its intellect. He had been born at Palermo, " the city of three tongues "; therefore Greek, Latin, and Arabic were equally familiar. He was daring in speech, broad in views, and cosmopolitan in habit. He founded the University of Naples and encouraged the study of medicine; he had the Greek of Aristotle translated, and himself set the fashion in verse-making, which was soon to be the pastime of every court in Italy.

The Pope was more successful in a contest waged with tongues than he had proved on battle-fields, which were strewn with bodies of both Guelf and Ghibelline factions. He dined in 1230 at the same table as his foe, but the peace between them did not long continue. In turn they triumphed, bringing against each other two armies of the Cross, the followers of the Pope fighting under the standard of St Peter's Keys as the champion of the true Christian Church against its oppressors.

Pope Innocent IV, who succeeded Gregory, proved himself a very cunning adversary. He might have won an easy victory over Frederick II if the exactions of the Papacy had not angered the countries where he sought refuge after his first failures. It was futile to declare at Lyons that the Emperor was deposed when all France was crying out upon the greed of prelates. The wearisome strife went on till the very peasants had to be guarded at their work by knights, sent out from towns to see that they were not taken captive. It was the day of the robber, and all things lay to his hand if he were bold enough to grasp them. Prisoners of war suffered horrible tortures, being hung up by their feet and hands in the hope that their friends would ransom them the sooner. Villages were burned down, and wolves howled near the haunts of men, seeking food to appease their ravening hunger. It was said that fierce beasts gnawed through the walls of houses and devoured little children in their cradles. Italy was rent by a conflict which divided one province from another, and even placed inhabitants of the same town on opposite sides and caused dissension in the noblest families.

The Flagellants marched in procession through the land, calling for peace but bringing tumult. The Emperor's party made haste to shut them out of the territory they ruled, but they could not rid the people of the terrible fear inspired by the barefooted, black-robed figures, with branches and candles in their hands and the holy Cross flaming red before them.

One defeat after another brought the House of Hohenstaufen under the control of the Church they had defied so boldly. Frederick's own son rebelled against him, and Frederick's camp was destroyed by a Guelf army. The Emperor had lived splendidly, making more impression on world-history than any other prince of that illustrious family, but he died in an hour of failure, feeling bitterly how great a triumph his death would be to the Pope who had conquered.

It was late in the year 1250 when the tidings of Frederick II's death travelled slowly through his Empire. Many refused to believe them, and declared long years afterwards that the Emperor was still living, beneath a mighty mountain. The world seemed to be shaking yet with the vibration of that deadly struggle. Conrad and Conradin were left, and Manfred, the favourite son of Frederick, but their reigns were short and desperate, and when they, too, had passed the Middle Ages were merging into another era. The "two swords" of Papacy and Empire were still to pierce and wound, but the struggle between them would never seem so mighty after the spirit had fled which inspired Conradin, last of the House of Swabia.

This young prince was led to the scaffold, where he asserted stoutly his claim to Naples above the claim of Charles, the Count of Anjou, who held it as fief of the Papacy. Then Conradin dared to throw his glove among the people, bidding them to carry it to Peter, Prince of Aragon, as the symbol by which he conveyed the rights of which death alone had been able to despoil him

Chapter II

Dante, the Divine Poet

THERE were still Guelfs and Ghibellines in 1265, but the old names had partially lost their meaning in the Republic of Florence, where the citizens brawled daily, one faction against the other. The nobles had, nevertheless, a bond with the emperor, being of the same Teutonic stock, and the burghers often sought the patronage of a very powerful pope, hoping in this way to maintain their well-loved independence.

But often Guelf and Ghibelline had no interest in anything outside the walls of Florence. The Florentine blood was hot and rose quickly to avenge insult. Family feuds were passionately upheld in a community so narrow and so zealous. If a man jostled another in the street, it was an excuse for a fight which might end in terrible bloodshed. Fear of banishment was no restraint to the combatants. The Guelf party would send away the Ghibelline after there had been some shameful tumult. Then the *fuori* (outside) were recalled because their own faction was in power again, and, in turn, the Guelfs were banished by the Ghibellines. In 1260 there had even been some talk of destroying the famous town in Tuscany. Florence would have been razed to the ground had not a party leader, Farinata degli Uberti, showed unexpected patriotism which saved her.

Florence had waxed mighty through her commerce,

holding a high place among the Italian cities which had thrown off the feudal yoke and become republics. Wealth gave the citizens leisure to study art and literature, and to attain to the highest civilization of a thriving state. The Italians of that time were the carriers of Europe, and as such had intercourse with every nation of importance. They were especially successful as bankers, Florentine citizens of middle rank acquiring such vast fortunes by finance that they outstripped the nobles who dwelt outside the gates and spent all their time in fighting. The guilds of Florence united men of the same trade and also encouraged perfection in the various branches. Goldsmiths offered marvellous wares for the purchase of the affluent dilettante. Silk was a natural manufacture, and paper had to be produced in a place where the School of Law attracted foreign scholars.

Rome had the renown of past splendour and the purple of imperial pride. Venice was the depôt of the world's trade, and sent fleets east and west laden with precious cargoes, which gave her a unique position among the five Republics. Bologna drew students from every capital in Europe to her ancient Universities. Milan had been a centre of learning even in the days of Roman rule, and the Emperor Maximilian had made it the capital of Northern Italy. Florence, somewhat overshadowed by such fame, could yet boast the most ancient origin. Was not Fæsulæ, lying close to her, the first city built when the Flood had washed away the abodes of men and left the earth quite desolate? *Fia sola*—" Let her be alone "—the words re-echoed through the whole neighbourhood and were the pride of Florence, which lay in a smiling fertile plain where all things flourished. The Florentines were coming to their own as the Middle Ages passed; they were people of cunning hand and brain, always eager to make money and spend it to procure the luxury and beauty their natures craved. The "florin" owed its popularity to the soundness of trade within the very streets where the bell, known as "the great cow," rang so lustily to summon the citizens to combat. The golden coins carried the repute of the fair Italian town to other lands, and changed owners so often that her prosperity was obvious.

Florence looked very fair when Durante Alighieri came into the world, for he was born on a May morning, and the Florentines were making holiday. There was mirth and jesting within the tall grey houses round the little church of San Martino The Alighieri dwelt in that quarter, but more humbly than their fine neighbours, the Portinari, the Donati, and the Cerci.

The Portinari celebrated May royally in 1275, inviting all their friends to a blithe gathering. At this *festa* Dante Alighieri met Beatrice, the little daughter of his host, and the long dream of his life began, for he idealized her loveliness from that first youthful meeting.

"Her dress on that day was of a most noble colour, a subdued and goodly crimson, girdled and adorned in such sort as best suited with her very tender age. At that moment I say most truly that the spirit of life, which hath its dwelling in the secretest chamber of the heart, began to tremble so violently that the least pulses of my body shook therewith; and in trembling it said these words—'*Ecce Deus fortior me, qui veniens dominabitur mihi.*' From that time Love ruled my soul. . . ."

Henceforth, Dante watched for the vision of Beatrice, weaving about her all the poetic fancies of his youth. He must have seen her many times, but no words passed between them till nine years had sped and he chanced to come upon her in all the radiance of her womanhood. She was " between two gentle ladies who were older than she ; and passing by in the street, she turned her eyes towards that place where I stood very timidly, and in her ineffable courtesy saluted me so graciously that I seemed then to see the heights of all blessedness. And because this was the first time her words came to my ears, it was so sweet to me that, like one intoxicated, I left all my companions, and retiring to the solitary refuge of my chamber I set myself to think of that most courteous one, and thinking of her, there fell upon me a sweet sleep, in which a marvellous vision appeared to me." The poet described the vision in verse—it was Love carrying a sleeping lady in one arm and in the other the burning heart of Dante. He wished that the sonnet he wrote should be answered by " all the faithful followers of love," and was gratified by the prompt reply of Guido Cavalcanti, who had won renown as a knight and minstrel.

Dante became the friend of this elder poet, and was encouraged to pursue his visionary history of the earlier years of his life and his fantastic adoration for Beatrice Portinari. The *Vita Nuova* was read by the poet's circle, who had a sympathetic interest in the details of the drama. The young lover did not confess his love to " the youngest of the angels," but he continued to worship her long after she had married Simone de Bardi.

Yet Dante entered into the ruder life of Florence, and took up arms for the Guelf faction, to which his family belonged. He fought in 1289 at the battle of Campaldino against the city of Arezzo and the Ghibellines who had taken possession of that city. Florence had been strangely peaceful in his childhood because the Guelfs were her unquestioned masters at the time. It must have

Dante in the Streets of Florence
Evelyn Paul

been a relief to Florentines to go forth to external warfare!

Dante played his part valiantly on the battle-field, then returned to wonderful aloofness from the strife of factions. He was stricken with grave fears that Beatrice must die, and mourned sublimely when the sad event took place on the ninth day of one of the summer months of 1290. "In their ninth year they had met, nine years after, they had spoken; she died on the ninth day of the month and the ninetieth year of the century."

Real life began with the poet's marriage when he was twenty-eight, for he allied himself to the noble Donati by marrying Gemma of that house. Little is known of the wife, but she bore seven children and seems to have been devoted. Dante still had his spiritual love for Beatrice in his heart, and planned a wonderful poem in which she should be celebrated worthily.

Dante began to take up the active duties of a citizen in 1293 when the people of Florence rose against the nobles and took all their political powers from them. The aristocratic party had henceforth to submit to the humiliation of enrolling themselves as members of some guild or art if they wished to have political rights in the Republic. The poet was not too proud to adopt this course, and was duly entered in the register of the art of doctors and apothecaries. It was not necessary that he should study medicine, the regulation being a mere form, probably to carry out the idea that every citizen possessing the franchise should have a trade of some kind.

The prosperity of the Republic was not destroyed by this petty revolution. Churches were built and stones laid for the new walls of Florence. Relations with other states demanded the services of a gracious and tactful embassy. Dante became an ambassador, and was successful in arranging the business of diplomacy and in promoting the welfare of his city. He was too much engaged in important affairs to pay attention to every miserable quarrel of the Florentines. The powerful Donati showed dangerous hostility now to the wealthy Cerchi, their near neighbours. Dante acted as a mediator when he could spare the time to hear complaints. He was probably more in sympathy with the popular cause which was espoused by the Cerchi than with the arrogance of his wife's family.

The feud of the Donati and Cerchi was fostered by the irruption of a family from Pistoia, who had separated into two distinct branches—the Bianchi and the Neri (the Whites and the Blacks)—and drawn their swords upon each other. The Cerchi chose to believe that the Bianchi were in the right, and, of course, the Donati took up the cause of the Neri. The original dispute had long been forgotten, but any excuse would serve two factions anxious to fight. Brawling took place at a May *festa*, in which several persons were wounded.

Dante was glad to divert his mind from all his discords when the last year of the thirteenth century came and he set out to Rome on pilgrimage. At Easter all the world seemed to be flocking to that solemn festival of the Catholic Church, where the erring could obtain indulgence by fifteen days of devotion. Yet the very break in the usual life of audiences and journeys must have been grateful to the tired ambassador. He began to muse on the poetic aims of his first youth and the work which was to make Beatrice's name immortal. Some lines of the new poem were written in the Latin tongue, then held the finest language for expressing a great subject. The poet had to abandon his scheme for a time at least, when he was made one of the Priors, or supreme rulers, of Florence in June 1300.

There was some attempt during Dante's brief term of office to settle the vexed question of the rival parties. Both deserved punishment, without doubt, and received it in the form of banishment for the heads of the factions. "Dante applied all his genius and every act and thought to bring back unity to the republic, demonstrating to the wiser citizens how even the great are destroyed by discord, while the small grow and increase infinitely when at peace. . . ."

Apparently Dante was not always successful in his attempts to unite his fellow-citizens. He talked of resignation sometimes and retirement into private life, a proposal which was opposed by his friends in office. When the losing side decided to ask Pope Boniface for an arbitrator to settle their disputes, all Dante's spirit rose against their lack of patriotism. He went willingly on an embassy to desire that Charles, the brother or cousin of King Philip of France, who had been selected to regulate the state of Florence, should come with a friendly feeling to his party, if his arrival could not be averted. He remained at Rome with other ambassadors for some unknown cause, while his party at Florence was defeated and sentence of banishment was passed on him as on the other leaders.

Dante loved the city of his birth and was determined to return from exile. He joined the band of *fuor-usciti*, or "turned-out," who were at that time plotting to reverse their fortunes. He cared not whether they were Guelf or Ghibelline in his passionate eagerness to win them to decisive action that would restore him to his rights as a Florentine citizen. He had no scruples in seeking foreign aid against the unjust Florentines. An armed attempt was made against Florence through his fierce endeavours, but it failed, as also a second conspiracy within three years, and by 1304 the poet had been seized with disgust of his companions outside the gates. He turned from them and went to the University of Bologna.

Dante's wife had remained in Florence, escaping from dangers, perhaps, because she belonged to the powerful family of Donati. Now she sent her eldest son, Pietro, to his father, with the idea that he should begin his studies at the ancient seat of learning.

After two years of a quiet life, spent in writing his *Essay on Eloquence* and reading philosophy, the exile was driven away from Bologna and had to take refuge with a noble of the Malespina family. He hated to receive patronage, and was thankful to set to work on his incomplete poem of the *Inferno*, which was sent to him from Florence. The weariness of exile was forgotten as he wrote the great lines that were to ring through the centuries and prove what manner of man his fellow-citizens had cast forth through petty wish for revenge and jealous hatred. He had written beautiful poems in his youth, telling of love and chivalry and fair women. Now he took the next world for his theme and the sufferings of those whose bodies have passed from earth and whose souls await redemption. "Where I am sailing none has tracked the sea" were his words, avowing an intention to forsake the narrower limits of all poets before him.

> "In the midway of this our mortal life,
> I found one in a gloomy wood, astray
> Gone from the path direct; and e'en to tell
> It were no easy task, how savage wild
> That forest, how robust and rough its growth,
> Which to remember only, my dismay
> Renews, in bitterness not far from death."

So the poet descended in imagination to the underworld, which he pictured reaching in wide circles from a vortex of sin and misery to a point of godlike ecstasy. With Vergil as a guide, he passed through the dark portals with their solemn warning.

> "Through me men pass to city of great woe,
> Through me men pass to endless misery,
> Through me men pass where all the lost ones go."

In 1305 the *Inferno* was complete, and Dante left it with the monks of a certain convent while he wandered into a far-distant country. The Frate questioned him eagerly, asking why he had chosen to write the poem in Italian since the vulgar tongue seemed to clothe such a wonderful theme unbecomingly. "When I considered the condition of the present age," the poet replied, "I saw that the songs of the most illustrious poets were neglected of all, and for this reason high-minded men who once wrote on such themes now left (oh! pity) the liberal arts to the crowd. For this I laid down the pure lyre with which I was provided and prepared for myself another more adapted to the understanding of the moderns. For it is vain to give sucklings solid food."

Dante fled Italy and again sat on the student's "bundle of straw," choosing Paris as his next refuge. There he discussed learned questions with the wise men of France, and endured much privation as well as the pangs of yearning for Florence, his beloved city, which seemed to forget him. Hope rose within his breast when the newly-elected Emperor, Henry of Luxemburg, resolved to invade Italy and pacify the rebellious spirit of the proud republics. Orders were given that Florence should settle her feuds once for all, but the Florentines angrily refused to acknowledge the imperial authority over their affairs and, while recalling a certain number of the exiled, refused to include the name of Dante.

Dante, in his fierce resentment, urged the Emperor to besiege the city which resisted his imperial mandates. The assault was unsuccessful, and Henry of Luxemburg died without accomplishing his laudable intention of making Italy more peaceful.

Dante lived under the protection of the powerful Uguccione, lord of Pisa, while he wrote the *Purgatorio*. The second part of his epic dealt with the region lying between the under-world of torment and the heavenly heights of Paradise itself. Here the souls of men were to be cleansed of their sins that they might be pure in their final ecstasy.

A revolt against his patron led the poet to follow him to Verona, where they both dwelt in friendship with the young prince, Cane della Scala. The later cantos of the great poem, the *Divine Comedy*, were sent to this ruler as they were written. Cane loved letters, and appreciated Dante so generously that the exile, for a time, was moved to forget his bitterness. He dedicated the *Paradiso* to della Scala, but he had to give up the arduous task of glorifying Beatrice worthily and devote himself to some humble office at Verona. The inferiority of his position galled one who claimed Vergil and Homer as his equals in the world of letters. He lost all his serene tranquillity of soul, and his face betrayed the haughty impatience of his spirit. Truly he was not the fitting companion for the buffoons and jesters among whom he was too often compelled to sit in the palaces where he accepted bounty. He could not always win respect by the power of his dark and piercing eyes, for he had few advantages of person and disdained to be genial in manners. Brooding over neglect and injustice, he grew so repellant that Cane was secretly relieved when thoughtless, cruel levity drove the poet from his court. He never cared, perhaps, that Dante, writing the concluding cantos of his poem, decided sadly not to send them to his former benefactor.

The last goal of Dante's wanderings was the ancient city of Ravenna, where his genius was honoured by the great, and he derived a melancholy pleasure from the wonder of the people, who would draw aside from his path and whisper one to another: "Do you see him who goes to hell and comes back again when he pleases?" The fame of the *Divine Comedy* was known to all, and men were amazed by the splendid audacity of the *Inferno*.

Yet Dante was still an exile when death took him in 1321, and Florence had stubbornly refused to pay him tribute. He was buried at Ravenna, and over his tomb in the little chapel an inscription reproached his own city with indifference.

"*Hic claudor Dantes patriis extorris ab oris,
Quem genuit parvi Florentia mater amoris.*"

"Here I am enclosed, Dante, exiled from my native country,
Whom Florence bore, the mother that little did love him."

Chapter III

Lorenzo the Magnificent

THE struggle in which Dante had played a leading part did not cease for many years after the poet had died in exile. The Florentines proved themselves so unable to rule their own city that they had to admit foreign control and bow before the Lords Paramount who came from Naples. The last of these died in 1328 and was succeeded by the Duke of Athens. This tyrant roused the old spirit of the people which had asserted its independence in former days. He was driven out of Florence on Saint Anne's Day, July 26th of 1343, and the anniversary of that brave fight for liberty was celebrated henceforth with loud rejoicing.

The *Ciompi*, or working-classes, rose in 1378 and demanded higher wages. They had been grievously oppressed by the nobles, and were encouraged by a general spirit of revolt which affected the peasantry of Europe. They were strong enough in Florence to set up a new government with one of their own rank as chief magistrate. But democracy did not enjoy a lengthy rule and the rich merchant-class came into power. Such families as the Albizzi and Medici were well able to buy the favour of the people.

There had been a tradition that the Florentine banking-house of Medici were on the popular side in those struggles which rent Florence. They were certainly born leaders and understood very thoroughly the nature of their turbulent fellow-citizens. They gained influence steadily during the sway of their rivals, the illustrious Albizzi. When Cosimo dei Medici had been banished, it was significant that the same convention of the people which recalled him should send Rinaldo degli Albizzi into exile.

Cosimo dei Medici rid himself of enemies by the unscrupulous method of his predecessors, driving outside the walls the followers of any party that opposed him. He had determined to control the Florentines so cleverly that they should not realize his tyranny. He was quite willing to spend the hoards of his ancestors on the adornment of the state he governed, and, among other things, he built the famous convent of St Mark. Fra Angelico, the painter-monk, was given the work of covering its white walls with the frescoes in which the monks delighted.

Cosimo gained thereby the reputation of liberality and gracious interest in the development of genius. The monk had devoted his time before this to the illuminations of manuscripts, and was delighted to work for the glory of God in such a way that all the convent might behold it. He wished for neither profit not praise for himself, but he knew that his beautiful vision would be inherited by his Church, and that they might inspire others of his brethren.

The Golden Age of Italian art was in its heyday under Cosimo dei Medici. Painters and architects had not been disturbed by the tumults that drew the rival factions from their daily labours. They had been constructing marvellous edifices in Florence even during the time when party feeling ran so high that it would have sacrificed the very existence of the city to its rancours.

The noble Cathedral had begun to rise before Dante had been banished, but there was no belfry till 1334 when Giotto laid the foundation-stone of the *Campanile*, whence the bells would ring through many centuries. The artist had completed his masterpiece in 1387, two years before the birth of Cosimo. It was an incentive to patriotic Florentines to add to the noble buildings of their city. The Church of San Lorenzo owed its existence to the House of Medici, which appealed to the people by lavish appreciation of all genius.

Cosimo was a scholar and welcomed the learned Greeks who fled from Constantinople when that city was taken by the Turks in 1453. He founded a Platonic Academy in Florence so that his guests were able to discuss philosophy at leisure. He professed to find consolation for all the misfortunes of his life in the writings of the Greek Plato, and read them rather ostentatiously in hours of bereavement. He collected as many classical manuscripts as his agents could discover on their journeys throughout Europe, and had these translated for the benefit of scholars. He had been in the habit of conciliating Alfonso of Naples by a present of gold and jewels, but as soon as a copy of Livy, the Latin historian, came to his hand, he sent the priceless treasure to his ally, knowing that the Neapolitan prince had an enormous reverence for learning. Cosimo, in truth, never coveted such finds for his own private use, but was always generous in exhibiting them at public libraries. He bought works of art to encourage the ingenuity of Florentine craftsmen, and would pay a high price for any new design, because he liked to think that his benevolence added to the welfare of the city.

Cosimo protected the commercial interests of Florence, identifying them with his own. He knew that peace was essential to the foreign trade, and tried to keep on friendly terms with the neighbours whose hostility would have destroyed it. He lived with simplicity in private life, but he needed wealth to maintain his position as patron of art and the New Learning; nor did he grudge the money which was scattered profusely to provide the gorgeous spectacles, beloved by the unlearned. He knew that nothing would rob the Florentines so easily of their ancient love of liberty as the experience of sensuous delights, in which all southern races find some satisfaction. He entertained the guests of the Republic with magnificence, that they might be impressed by the security of his unlawful government.

Lorenzo, the grandson of Cosimo dei Medici, carried on his policy. It had been successful, for the Florentines of their own accord put themselves beneath the sway of a second tyrant.

" Poets of every kind, gentle and simple, with golden cithern and with rustic lute, came from every quarter to animate the suppers of the Magnifico; whosoever sang of arms, of love, of saints, of fools, was welcome, or he who, drinking and joking, kept the company amused. . . . And in order that the people might not be excluded from this new beatitude (a thing which was important to the Magnifico), he composed and set in order many mythological representations, triumphal cars, dances, and every kind of festal celebration, to solace and delight them; and thus he succeeded in banishing from their souls any recollection of their ancient greatness, in making them insensible to the ills of the country, in disfranchising and debasing them by means of temporal ease and intoxication of the senses."

Lorenzo the Magnificent was endowed with charms

that were naturally potent with a beauty-loving people. He had been very carefully trained by the prudent Cosimo, so that he excelled in physical exercises and could also claim a place among the most intellectual in Florence. Although singularly ill-favoured, he had personal qualities which attracted men and women. He spared no pains to array himself with splendour whenever he appeared in public. At tournaments he wore a costume ornamented with gold and silver thread, and displayed the great Medicean diamond—*Il Libro*—on his shield, which bore the *fleur-de-lis* of France in token of the friendship between the Medici and that nation. The sound of drums and fifes heralded the approach of Lorenzo the Magnificent, and cheers acclaimed him victor when he left the field bearing the coveted silver helmet as a trophy.

Lorenzo worshipped a lady who had given him a bunch of violets as a token, according to the laws of chivalry. He wrote sonnets in honour of Lucrezia Donati, but he was not free to marry her, the great house of Medici looking higher than her family. The bride, chosen for the honour of mating with the ruler of Florence, was a Roman lady of such noble birth that it was not considered essential that she should bring a substantial dowry. Clarice Orsini was dazzled at her wedding-feast by the voluptuous splendour of the family which she entered.

The ceremony took place at Florence in 1469 and afforded an excuse for lavish hospitality. The bride received her own guests in the garden of the villa where she was to reign as mistress. Young married women surrounded her, admiring the costliness of her clothing and preening themselves in the rich attire which they had assumed for this great occasion. In an upper room of the villa the bridegroom's mother welcomed her own friends of mature years, and listened indulgently to the sounds of mirth that floated upward from the cloisters of the courtyard. Lorenzo sat there with the great Florentines who had assembled to honour his betrothal. The feast was served with solemnity at variance with the wit and laughter that were characteristic of the gallant company. The blare of trumpets heralded the arrival of dishes, which were generally simple. The stewards and carvers bowed low as they served the meats; their task was far from light since abundance was the rule of the house of Medici. No less than five thousand pounds of sweetmeats had been provided for the wedding, but it must be remembered that the banquets went on continuously for several days, and the humblest citizen could present himself at the hospitable boards of the bridegroom and his kinsfolk. The country-folk had sent the usual gifts of fat hens and capons, and were greeted with a welcome as gracious as that bestowed on the guests whose offerings were rings or brocades or costly illuminated manuscripts.

After his marriage, Lorenzo was called upon to undertake a foreign mission. He travelled to Milan and there stood sponsor to the child of the reigning Duke, Galeazzo Sforza, in order to cement an alliance. He gave a gold collar, studded with diamonds, to the Duchess of Milan, and answered as became him when she was led to express the hope that he would be godfather to all her children! It was Lorenzo's duty to act as host when the Duke of Milan came to visit Florence. He was not dismayed by the long train of attendants which followed the Duke, for he knew that these richly-dressed warriors might be bribed to fight for his State if he conciliated their master. There were citizens in Florence, however, who shrank from the barbaric ostentation of their ally. They looked upon a fire which broke out in a church as a divine denunciation of the mystery play performed in honour of their guests, and were openly relieved to shut their gates upon the Duke of Milan and his proud forces.

Lorenzo betrayed no weakness when the town of Volterra revolted against Florence, which exercised the rights of a protector. He punished the inhabitants very cruelly, banishing all the leaders of the revolt and taking away the Volterran privilege of self-government. His enemies hinted that he behaved despotically in order to secure certain mineral rights in this territory, and held him responsible for the sack of Volterra, though he asserted that he had gone to offer help to such of the inhabitants as had lost everything.

But the war of the Pazzi conspiracy was the true test of the strength of Medicean government. It succeeded a time of high prosperity in Florence, when her ruler was honoured by the recognition of many foreign powers, and felt his position so secure that he might safely devote much leisure to the congenial study of poetry and philosophy.

Between the years 1474-8 Lorenzo had managed to incur the jealous hatred of Pope Sixtus IV, who was determined to become the greatest power in Christendom. This Pontiff skilfully detached Naples from her alliance with Florence and Milan by promising to be content with a nominal tribute of two white horses every year instead of the handsome annual sum she had usually exacted from this vassal. He congratulated himself especially on this stroke of policy, because he believed Venice to be too selfish as a commercial State to combine with her Italian neighbours and so form another Triple Alliance. He then proceeded to win over the Duke of Urbino, who had been the leader of the Florentine army. He also thwarted the ambition of Florentine trade by purchasing the tower of Imola from Milan. The Medici, coveting the bargain for their traffic with the East, were too indignant to advance the money which, as bankers to the Papacy, they should have supplied. They preferred to see their rivals, the great Roman banking-house of the Pazzi, accommodating the Pope, even though this might mean a fatal blow to their supremacy.

Lorenzo's hopes of a strong coalition against his foe were destroyed by the assassination of Sforza of Milan in 1474. The Duke was murdered in the church of St Stephen by three young nobles who had personal injuries to avenge and were also inspired by an ardent desire for republican liberty. The Pope exclaimed, when he heard the news, that the peace of Italy was banished by this act of lawlessness. Lorenzo, disapproving of all outbreaks against tyranny, promised to support the widowed Duchess of Milan. The control he exercised during her brief régime came to an end in 1479 with the usurpation of Ludovico, her Moorish brother-in-law.

Then Riario, the Pope's nephew, saw that the time was ripe for a conspiracy against the Medici which might deprive them of their power in Italy. He allied himself closely with Francesco dei Pazzi, who was anxious for the aggrandisement of his own family. His name had long been famous in Florence, every good citizen watching the ancient *Carro dei Pazzi* which was borne in procession at Easter-tide. The car was stored with fireworks set alight by means of the *Colombina* (Dove) bringing a spark struck from a stone fragment of Christ's tomb. The citizens could not forget the origin of the sacred flame, for they had all heard in youth the story of the return of a crusading member of the Pazzi house with that precious relic.

The two conspirators hoped to bring a foreign army against Florence and, therefore, gained the aid of Salviati, Archbishop of Pisa. The Pope bade them do as they wished, "provided that there be no killing." In reality, he was aware that a plot to assassinate both Lorenzo dei Medici and his brother, Giuliano, was on foot, but considered that it would degrade his holy office if he spoke of it.

It was necessary for their first plan that Lorenzo should be lured to Rome where the conspirators had assembled, but he refused an invitation to confer with the Pope about their differences and a new plan had to be substituted. Accordingly the nephew of Riario, Cardinal Raffaelle Sansoni, expressed a keen desire to view the treasures of the Medici household, and was welcomed as a guest by Florence. He attended mass in the Cathedral which was to be the scene of the assassination, since Lorenzo and his brother were certain to attend it. Two priests offered to perform the deed of sacrilege from which the original assassin recoiled. They hated Lorenzo for his treatment of Volterra, and drove him behind the gates of the new sacristy. Giuliano was slain at the very altar, his body being pierced with no less than nineteen wounds, but Lorenzo escaped to mourn the fate of the handsome noble brother who had been a model for Botticelli's famous "Primavera."

He heard the citizens cry, "Down with traitors! The Medici! The Medici!" and resolved to move them to a desperate vengeance on the Pazzi. The Archbishop of Pisa was hanged from the window of a palace, while a fellow-conspirator was hurled to the ground from the same building. This gruesome scene was painted to gratify the avengers of Giuliano.

Florence was enthusiastic in defence of her remaining tyrant. He was depicted by Botticelli in an attitude of triumph over the triple forces of anarchy, warfare and sedition. All the family of Pazzi were condemned as traitors. Their coat of arms was erased by Lorenzo's adherents wherever it was discovered.

Henceforth, Lorenzo exercised supreme control over his native city. He won Naples to a new alliance by a diplomatic visit that proved his skill in foreign negotiations. The gifts that came to him from strange lands were presented, in reality, to the master of the Florentine "republic." Egypt sent a lion and a giraffe, which were welcomed as wonders of the East even by those who did not appreciate the fact that they showed a desire to trade. It was easy soon to find new markets for the rich burghers whose class was in complete ascendancy over the ancient nobles.

Lorenzo was seized with mortal sickness in the early spring of 1492, and found no comfort in philosophy. He drank from a golden cup which was supposed to revive the dying when it held a draught, strangely concocted from precious pearls according to some Eastern fancy. But the sick man found nothing of avail in his hour of death except a visit from an honest monk he had seen many times in the cloisters of San Marco.

Savonarola came to the bedside of the magnificent pagan and demanded three things as the price of absolution. Lorenzo was to believe in the mercy of God, to restore all that he had wrongfully acquired, and to agree to popular government being restored to Florence. The third condition was too hard, for Lorenzo would not own himself a tyrant. He turned his face to the wall in bitterness of spirit, and the monk withdrew leaving him unshriven

The sack of Volterra, and the murder of innocent kinsfolk of the Pazzi who had been involved in the great conspiracy haunted Lorenzo as he passed from life in the prime of manhood and glorious achievements. He would have mourned for the commerce of his city if he had known that in the same year of 1492 the discovery of America would be made, through which the Atlantic Ocean was to become the highway of commerce, reducing to sad inferiority the ports of the Mediterranean.

Chapter IV

The Prior of San Marco

LONG before Lorenzo's death, Girolamo Savonarola had made the corruption of Florence the subject of sermons which drew vast crowds to San Marco. The city might pride herself on splendid buildings decorated by the greatest of Italian painters; she might rouse envy in the foreign princes who were weary of listening to the praises of Lorenzo; but the preacher lamented the sins of Florentines as one of old had lamented the wickedness of Nineveh, and prophesied her downfall if the pagan lust for enjoyment did not yield to the sternest Christianity.

Savonarola had witnessed many scenes which showed the real attitude of the Pope toward religion. He had been born at Ferrara, where the extravagant and sumptuous court had extended a flattering welcome to Pius IV as he passed from town to town to preach a Crusade against the Turks. The Pope was sheltered by a golden canopy and greeted by sweet music, and statues of heathen gods were placed on the river-banks as an honour to the Vicar of Christ!

Savonarola shrank from court-life and the patronage of Borsi, the reigning Marquis of Ferrara. That prince, famed for his banquets, his falcons, and his robes of gold brocade, would have appointed him the court physician if he would have agreed to study medicine.

The study of the Scriptures appealed more to the recluse, whose only recreation was to play the lute and write verses of a haunting melancholy.

Against the wishes of his family Savonarola entered the Order of Saint Dominic. He gave up the world for a life of the hardest service in the monastery by day, and took his rest upon a coarse sack at night. He was conscious of a secret wish for pre-eminence, no doubt, even when he took the lowest place and put on the shabbiest clothing.

The avarice of Pope Sextus roused the monk to burning indignation. The new Pope lavished gifts on his own family, who squandered on luxury of every kind the money that should have relieved the poor. The Church seemed to have entered zealously into that contest for wealth and power which was devastating all the free states of Italy.

Savonarola had come from his monastery at Bologna to the Convent of San Marco when he first lifted up his voice in denunciation. He was not well received because he used the Bible—distrusted by the Florentines, who expressed doubts of the correctness of its Latin! Pico della Mirandola, the brilliant young scholar, was attracted, however, by the friar's eloquence. A close friendship was formed between these two men, whose appearance was as much in contrast as their characters.

Savonarola was dark in complexion, with thick lips and an aquiline nose—only the flashing grey eyes set under overhanging brows redeemed his face from harshness. Mirandola, on the other hand, was gifted with remarkable personal beauty. Long fair curls hung to his shoulders and surrounded a face that was both gentle and gracious. He had an extraordinary knowledge of languages and a wonderful memory.

The Prior of San Marco

Fastidious Florentines were converted to Mirandola's strange taste in sermons, so that the convent garden with its rose-trees became the haunt of an ever-increasing crowd, eager to hear doctrines which were new enough to tickle their palates pleasantly. On the 1st of August 1489, the friar consented to preach in the Convent Church to the Dominican brothers and the laymen who continued to assemble in the cloisters. He took a passage of Revelations for his text. " Three things he suggested to the people. That the Church of God required renewal, and that immediately ; second, that all Italy should be chastised ; third, that this should come to pass soon." This was the first of Savonarola's prophecies, and caused great excitement among the Florentines who heard it.

At Siena, the preacher pronounced sentence on the Church, which was now under the rule of Innocent IV, a pope more openly depraved than any of his predecessors. Through Lombardy the echo of that sermon sounded and the name of Girolamo Savonarola. The monk was banished, and only recalled to Florence by the favour of Lorenzo dei Medici, who was undisturbed by a series of sermons against tyranny.

Savonarola was elected Prior of San Marco in July 1491, but he refused to pay his respects to Lorenzo as the patron of the convent. " Who elected me to be Prior—God or Lorenzo ? " he asked sternly when the elder Dominicans entreated him to perform this duty. " God," was the answer they were compelled to make. They were sadly disappointed when the new Prior decided, " Then I will thank my Lord God, not mortal man."

In the Lent season of this same year Savonarola preached for the first time in the cathedral or Duomo of Florence. "The people got up in the middle of the night to get places for the sermon, and came to the door of the cathedral, waiting outside till it should be opened, making no account of any inconvenience, neither of the cold nor the wind, nor of standing in the winter with their feet on the marble; and among them were young and old, women and children of every sort, who came with such jubilee and rejoicing that it was bewildering to hear them, going to the sermon as to a wedding. . . . And though many thousand people were thus collected together no sound was to be heard, not even a 'hush,' until the arrival of the children, who sang hymns with so much sweetness that heaven seemed to have opened."

The Magnificent often came to San Marco, piqued by the indifference of the Prior and interested in the personality of the man who had succeeded in impressing cultured Florentines by simple language. He gave gold pieces lavishly to the convent, but the gold was always sent to the good people of St Martin, who ministered to the needs of those who were too proud to acknowledge their decaying fortunes. "The silver and copper are enough for us," were the words that met the remonstrances of the other brethren. "We do not want so much money." No wonder that Lorenzo remembered the invincible honesty of this Prior when he was convinced of the hollowness of the life he had led among a court of flatterers!

The Prior's warnings were heard in Florence with an uneasy feeling that their fulfilment might be nearer after Lorenzo died and was succeeded by his son. Piero dei Medici sent the preacher away from the city, for he knew that men whispered among themselves that the Dominican had foretold truly the death of Innocent and the parlous state of Florence under the

The Prior of San Marco

new Pope, Alexander VI (Alexander Borgia). He did not like the predictions of evil for his own house of Medici, which had now wielded supreme power in Florence for over sixty years. It would go hardly with him if the people were to rise against the tyranny his fathers had established.

Piero's downfall was hastened by the news that a French army had crossed the Alps under Charles VIII of France, who intended to take Naples. This invasion of Italy terrified the Florentines, for they had become unwarlike since they gave themselves up to luxury and pleasure. They dreaded the arrival of the French troops, which were famous throughout Europe. On these Charles relied to intimidate the citizens of the rich states he visited on his way to enforce a claim transmitted to him through Charles of Anjou. Piero de Medici made concessions to the invader without the knowledge of the people. The Florentines rebelled against the admission of soldiers within their walls as soon as the advance guard arrived to mark with chalk the houses they would choose for their quarters. There were frantic cries of "*Abbasso le palle*," "Down with the balls," in allusion to the three balls on the Medici coat of arms. Piero himself was disowned and driven from the city.

All the enemies of the Medici were recalled, and the populace entreated Savonarola to return and protect them in their hour of peril. They had heard him foretell the coming of one who should punish the wicked and purge Italy of her sins. Now their belief in the Prior's utterances was confirmed. They hastened to greet him as the saviour of their city.

Savonarola went on an embassy to Charles' camp and made better terms than the Florentines had expected. Nevertheless, they had to endure the procession of French troops through their town, and found it difficult to get rid of Charles VIII, whose cupidity was aroused when he beheld the wealth of Florence. There was tumult in the streets, where soldiers brawled with citizens and enraged their hosts by insults. The Italian blood was greatly roused when the invading monarch threatened "to sound his trumpets" if his demands were not granted. "Then we will ring our bells," a bold citizen replied. The French King knew how quickly the town could change to a stronghold of barricaded streets if such an alarm were given, and wisely refrained from further provocation. He passed on his way after "looting" the palace in which he had been lodged. The Medicean treasures were the trophies of his visit.

In spite of himself, the monk had to turn politician after the French army had gone southward. He was said to have saved the State, and was implored to assume control now that the tyranny was at an end. There was a vision before him of Florence as a free Republic in the truest sense. He took up his work gladly for the cause of liberty. The *Parliamento*, a foolish assembly of the people which was summoned hastily to do the will of any faction that could overawe it, was replaced by the Great Council formed on a Venetian model. In this sat the *benefiziati*—those who had held some civic office, and the immediate descendants of officials. Florence was not to have a really democratic government.

After the cares of government, Savonarola felt weary in mind and body; he had never failed to preach incessantly in the cathedral, where he expounded his schemes for reform without abandoning his work as prophet. He broke down, but again took up his burden bravely. Florence was a changed city under his rule. Women clothed themselves in the simplest garb and forsook such vanities as wigs and rouge-pots. Bankers, repenting of greed, hastened to restore the wealth they had wrongly appropriated. Tradesmen read their Bibles in their shops in the intervals of business, and were no longer to be found rioting in the streets. The Florentine youths, once mischievous to the last degree, attended the friar daily, and actually gave up their stone-throwing. "*Piagnoni*" (Snivellers) was the name given to these enthusiasts, for the godly were not without opponents.

Savonarola had to meet the danger of an attempt to restore the authority of Piero dei Medici. He mustered eleven thousand men and boys, when a report came that the tyrant had sought the help of Charles VIII against Florence. The Pope, also, wished to restore Piero for his own ends. In haste the citizens barred their gates and then assembled in the cathedral to hearken to their leader.

Savonarola passed a stern resolution that any man should be put to death who endeavoured to destroy the hard-won freedom of his city. "One must treat these men," he declared, "as the Romans treated those who sought the recall of Tarquinius." His fiery spirit inflamed the Florentines with such zeal that they offered four thousand gold florins for the head of Piero dei Medici.

The attempt to force the gates of Florence proved a failure. Piero had to fly to Rome and the Prior's enemies were obliged to seek a fresh excuse for attacking his position. The Pope was persuaded to send for him that he might answer a charge of disseminating false doctrines. The preacher defended himself vigorously, and seemed to satisfy Alexander Borgia, whose aim was to crush a reformer of the Catholic Church likely to attack his evil practices. He was, however, forbidden to preach, and had to be silent at the time when Florence held her carnival.

The extraordinary change in the nature of this festival was a tribute to the influence of Savonarola. Children went about the streets, chanting hymns instead of the licentious songs which Lorenzo dei Medici had written for the purpose. They begged alms for the poor, and their only amusement was the *capannucci*, or Bonfire of Vanities, for which they collected the materials. Books and pictures, clothes and jewels, false hair and ointments were piled in great heaps round a kind of pyramid some sixty feet in height. Old King Carnival, in effigy, was placed at the apex of the pyramid, and the interior was filled with comestibles that would set the whole erection in a blaze as soon as a taper was applied. When the signal was given, bells pealed and trumpets sounded glad farewell to the customs of the ancient carnival. The procession set forth from San Marco on Palm Sunday (led by white-robed children with garlands on their heads), and went round the city till it came to the cathedral. "And so much joy was there in all hearts that the glory of Paradise seemed to have descended on earth and many tears of tenderness and devotion were shed." So readily did Florentines confess that the new spirit of Christianity brought more satisfaction than the noisy licence of a pagan festival.

In 1496 the Pope not only allowed Savonarola to preach, but even offered him a Cardinal's Hat on condition that he would utter no more predictions. "I want no other red hat but that of martyrdom, reddened

The Prior of San Marco

by my own blood," was the firm response of the incorruptible preacher. He was greeted by joyful shouts when he mounted to the pulpit of the Duomo, and had reached the height of his popularity in Florence.

When a year had passed, Savonarola faced a different world, where friends were fain to conceal their devotion and enemies became loud in their constant menaces. The *Arrabiati* (enraged) had overcome the *Piagnoni* and induced the Pope to pronounce excommunication against the leader of this party. The sermons continued, the Papal decree was ignored, but a new doubt had entered the mind of Florentines. A Franciscan monk, Francesco da Puglia, had attacked the Dominican, calling him a false prophet and challenging him to prove the truth of his doctrines by the "ordeal by fire."

Savonarola hesitated to accept the challenge, knowing that he would be destroyed by it, whatever might be the actual issue. The *Piagnoni* showed some chagrin when he allowed a disciple, Fra Domenico, to step into his place as a proof of devotion. On all sides there were murmurs at the Prior's strange shrinking and obvious reluctance to meet with a miracle the charges of his opponents.

A great crowd assembled on the day appointed for the "ordeal" in the early spring of 1498. Balconies and roofs were black with human figures, children clung to columns and statues in order that they might not lose a glimpse of this rare spectacle. Only a few followers of Savonarola prayed and wept in the Piazza of San Marco as the chanting procession of Domenicans appeared. Fra Domenico walked last of all, arrayed in a cope of red velvet to symbolize the martyr's flames. He did not fear to prove the strength of his belief, but walked erect and bore the cross in triumph. It was the

Franciscan brother whose courage failed for he had never thought, perhaps, that any man would be brave enough to reply to his awful challenge.

The crowd watched, feverishly expectant, but the hours passed and there was no sign of Francesco da Puglia. His brethren found fault with Domenico's red cope and bade him change it. They consulted, and came at last to the conclusion that their own champion had found himself unable to meet martyrdom. At length it was announced that there would be no ordeal—a thunderstorm had not caused one spectator to leave his place in the Piazza, where there should be wrought a miracle. It was clear that the Prior's enemies had sought his death, for they showed a furious passion of resentment. Even the *Piagnoni* were troubled by doubts of their prophet, who had refused to show his supernatural powers and silence the Franciscans. The monks were protected with difficulty from the violence of the mob as they returned in the April twilight to the Convent of San Marco.

There was the sound of vespers in the church when a noise of tramping feet was heard and the fierce cry, "To San Marco!" The monks rose from their knees to shut the doors through which assailants were fast pouring. These soldiers of the Cross fought dauntlessly with any weapon they could seize when they saw that their sacred dwelling was in danger.

Savonarola called the Dominicans round him and led them to the altar, where he knelt in prayer, commanding them to do likewise. But some of the white-robed brethren had youthful spirits and would not refrain from fighting. They rose and struggled to meet death, waving lighted torches about the heads of their assailants. A novice met naked swords with a great

The Last Sleep of Savonarola
Sir George Reid, P.R.S.A.

wooden cross he took to defend the choir from sacrilege. "Save Thy people, O God"; it was the refrain of the very psalm they had been singing. The place was dense with smoke, and the noise of the strife was deafening. A young monk died on the very altar steps, and received the last Sacrament from Fra Domenico amid this strange turmoil.

As soon as a pause came in the attack, Savonarola led the brethren to the library. He told them quietly that he was resolved to give himself up to his enemies that there might be no further bloodshed. He bade them farewell with tenderness and walked forth into the dangerous crowd about the convent. His hands were tied and he was beaten and buffeted on his way to prison. The first taste of martyrdom was bitter in his mouth, and he regretted that he had not answered the Franciscan's challenge.

The prophet was put on trial on a charge of heresy and sedition. He was tortured so cruelly that he was led to recant and to "confess," as his judges said. They had already come to a decision that he was guilty. Sentence of death was pronounced, and he mounted the scaffold on May 23rd, 1498. He looked upon the multitude gathered in the great Piazza, but he did not speak to them; he did not save himself, as some of them were hoping. It was many years before Florence paid him due honour as the founder of her liberties and the greatest of her reformers.

Chapter V

Martin Luther, Reformer of the Church

THE martyrdom of Savonarola gave courage to reformers and renewed the faith of the people. It had been his aim to progress steadily toward the truth and to draw the whole world after him. Unconsciously he prepared the way for the German monk who destroyed the unity of the Catholic Church. Though he was merciless to papal abuses, it had not been in the mind of the zealous Dominican to protest against the doctrines of the Papacy, nor did he ever doubt the faith which had drawn him to the convent. He had no wish to destroy —his work was to purify. But his death proved that purification was impossible. Rome had gone too far on the downward path to be checked by a Reformer. She had come at last to the parting of the ways.

Martin Luther knew nothing of the pomp of Italian cities. He was born in very humble circumstances at Eisleben, a little town in Germany, on St Martin's Eve, 1483. Harsh discipline made his childhood unhappy, for the age of educational reformers had not yet come. The little Martin was beaten and tormented, and had to sing in the streets for bread.

Ambition roused his parents to send him to the University of Erfurt that he might study law. He took his degree as Doctor of Philosophy in 1505—the event was celebrated by a torchlight procession and rejoicing, after the student-custom of those parts.

Then Martin Luther, appalled by the sudden death of a comrade in a thunderstorm, resolved to devote himself to God. Luther was a genial youth, and gave a supper to his friends before he left them; there were feasting and laughter and a burst of song. That same evening the door of a convent opened to receive a novice with two books, Vergil and Plautus, in his hand.

The novice had to perform the meanest tasks, sweeping floors and begging in the street on behalf of his brethren of the Augustinian Order. "Go through the street with a sack and get food for us," they clamoured, driving him out that they might resume their idleness.

Staupnitz, the head of the Order, visited the convent and was interested in the young man to whom fasting and penance did not bring the peace he craved. Oppressed by his sins, Luther lived a life of misery. He read the Bible constantly, having discovered the Holy Book by chance within the convent walls. At last, the words of the creed brought comfort to him "*I believe* in the forgiveness of sins." He despaired of his soul no longer. "It was as if I had found the door of Paradise wide open," he said joyfully, and devoted himself more closely to the study of the Scriptures.

The fame of Luther's learning spread beyond the convent of his Order. He was summoned to teach philosophy and theology at Wittenberg, a new university, founded by Frederick, the Elector of Saxony. The boldness of the lecturer's spirit was first shown in his sermons against "indulgences," one of the worst abuses of the Roman Church.

The Pope claimed to inherit the keys of St Peter,

which opened the treasury containing the good works of the saints and the boundless merits of Jesus Christ. He professed to be able to transfer a portion of this merit to any person who gave a sum of money to purchase pardon for sins. "Indulgences" had been first granted to pilgrims and Crusaders. They were further extended to those who aided pious works, such as the building of St Peter's. The Pope, Leo X, had found the papal treasury exhausted by his predecessors. He had to raise money, and therefore allowed agents to sell pardons throughout Germany. Tetzel, a Dominican friar, was employed in Saxony. He was noisy and dishonest, and spent on his own evil pleasures sums that were given by the ignorant creatures upon whom he traded to secure their eternal happiness.

Luther inveighed against such practices from the pulpit of the church at Wittenberg. He was particularly angry to hear Tetzel's wicked proclamation that "when one dropped a penny into the box for a soul in purgatory, so soon as the money chinked in the chest, the soul flew up to heaven."

The papal red cross hung above Tetzel's money-counter, and he sat there and called on all to buy. Luther decided on an action that should stop the shameful traffic, declaring, "God willing, I will beat a hole in his drum." On the eve of All Saints' Day a crowd assembled to gaze at the relics displayed at the Castle church of Wittenberg. Their attention was drawn to a paper nailed on the church gate, which set forth reasons why indulgences were harmful and should be immediately discontinued.

There were other abuses in the Church of Rome which Luther now openly deplored. Hot discussion followed this bold step. Tetzel retired to Frankfort,

Martin Luther

but from there he wrote to contradict the new teaching of the Augustine monk. He burnt Luther's theses publicly, and then heard that his own had been consigned to the flames in the market-place of Wittenberg, where a host of sympathisers had watched the bonfire with satisfaction. Luther did not stand alone in his struggle to free the Church from vice and superstition. He lived in an age when men had learning enough to despise the trickery of worldly monks. The spirit of inquiry had lived through the Revival of Letters and Erasmus, the famous scholar, had discovered many errors in the Roman Church.

Erasmus joined Luther in an attempt to show men that the Holy Scriptures alone would offer guidance in spiritual matters. He knew that a reform of the Western Church was urgently needed, and was willing to use his subtle brains to confute the arguments of ignorant opponents. But soon he found that Luther's temper was too ardent, that there was no middle course for this impetuous spirit. He dreaded for himself the loss of wealth and honour, and refused to make war on those in high stations, whose patronage had helped him to the rewards of knowledge.

Alarmed by the spread of Luther's books and doctrines, the cardinals entreated the Pope to summon him to Rome. Printing had been invented, and poor as well as rich could easily be roused to inquire into the truth of the doctrines taught by Rome. Leo X had been disposed to ignore the sermons of the obscure German monk, for he had many schemes to further his own ambition. He yielded, at last, and sent the necessary summons. Luther was loth to go to Rome, where he was sure of condemnation. The Elector Frederick of Saxony came forward as his champion, not from religious motives, but because he was pleased to see some prospect of the exactions of the court of Rome being diminished.

Cajetan, the Papal Legate, came to preside over a Diet, summoned specially to Augsburg. He urged the monk to retract his dangerous doctrine that the authority of the Bible was above that of the Pope of Rome. "Retract, my son, retract," he urged; "it is hard for thee to kick against the pricks." But the conference ended where it had begun—Luther fled back to Wittenberg.

He began to see now that the whole system of Romish government was wrong, and that there were countless abuses to be swept away before the Church could truly claim to point the way to Christianity. Conscience or authority, the Scriptures or the Church, Germany or Rome? A choice had to be made, each man ranging himself on one side or the other. The independence of Germany was dear to Luther's heart. He wrote an address to the nobles and summoned the Christian princes of Germany to his aid. He declared that all Christians were priests, and that the Church and nation ought to be freed from the interference of the Papacy. He was becoming an avowed enemy of the Pope, losing his former reluctance to attack authority. A Bull was, of course, issued against him, but the students of Erfurt threw the paper on which it was written into the river, saying contemptuously—"It is a bubble, let it swim!"

In December, 1520, Luther himself burnt the Bull on a fire kindled for the purpose at the Elster Gate of Wittenberg. He said, as he committed the document to the flames, "As thou hast vexed the saints of God, so mayest thou be consumed in eternal fire." The act cut him off from the Papacy for ever. He had defied the Pope in the presence of many witnesses.

Martin Luther

Charles V, the Holy Roman Emperor, was not in a position to take up the cause of Luther against his powerful enemies. He maintained an alliance with the Pope so that he would oppose the vast schemes which his rival, Francis I of France, was maturing. At the same time, he owed a debt of gratitude to the Elector Frederick, who was one of the seven German princes possessing the right to "elect" a new emperor. He decided, after a brief struggle, to yield to the demands of the Papal Legates. He ordered Martin Luther to come to Worms and appear before the great Diet, or Assembly of German rulers, which met in 1521.

Luther obeyed at once, making a triumphant journey through many towns and villages. Music fell on his ears pleasantly, a portrait of Savonarola was sent to him that he might feel his courage strengthened. Had not his resolve been fixed, he would have turned back at Weimar, where he found an edict posted on the walls ordering all his writings to be burnt. "I am lawfully called to appear in that city," he said, "and thither will I go in the name of the Lord, though as many devils as there are tiles on the houses were there combined against me." He was stricken with illness at Eisenach, but went on as soon as he recovered. When he caught sight of the old towers of Worms, his spirit leapt with joy, and he began to sing his famous hymn, "*Ein feste Burg ist unser Gott.*" ("A mighty fortress is our God.")

The crowded streets testified to the fame that had gone before him. Not even the Emperor had met with such a flattering reception. Saxon noblemen welcomed him, and friendly speech cheered him to meet the ordeal of the next day. The Diet was an impressive assembly, with the Emperor on his throne and the great dignitaries of State around him, clad in all the majesty of red and purple. Not the chivalry of Germany only had flocked to hear the defence of Martin Luther for Spanish warriors sat there in yellow cloaks and added lustre to the splendid gathering.

Luther's courageous stand against his adversaries won many to his cause. He would not withdraw one word he had written or spoken, nor did he consent to his opinions being tried by any other rule than the word of God.

Eric, the aged Duke of Brunswick, sent him a silver can of Einbech beer as a token of sympathy. Weary of strife, Luther drank it, saying, "As Duke Eric has remembered me this day, so may our Lord Christ remember him in his last struggle."

The reformer called in vain on the Emperor and States, assembled at Worms, to consider the parlous case of the Church, lest God should visit the German nation with His judgment. A severe edict was published against him by the authority of the Diet, and he was deprived of all the privileges he enjoyed as a subject of the Empire. Furthermore, it was forbidden for any prince to harbour or protect him, and his person was to be seized as soon as the safe-conduct for the journey had expired.

As Luther returned to Wittenberg, a band of horsemen took him and carried him off to the strong castle of Wartburg, where he was lodged in the disguise of a knight. It was a ruse of the Elector of Saxony to save him from the storm he had roused by his behaviour at the Diet. Imprisonment was not irksome, and the retreat was pleasant enough after the strife of years. He hunted in his character of gallant cavalier, and always wore a sword. Much of his time was spent in translating the Scriptures into German, that knowledge might not be denied even to the unlettered. Constant study made his imagination very vivid, and the devil seemed to be constantly before him. He had long conversations with Satan in person, as he believed, and decided that the best way to get rid of him was by gibes and mockery. One night his bed shook with the violent agitation caused by the rattling of some hazel nuts against each other after they had felt the inspiration of the Evil One! On another occasion a diabolical moth buzzed round him, preventing close attention to his labours. He hurled an inkstand at the intruder, staining the wall of the chamber with a mark that remained there through centuries.

During this confinement, Luther's opinions gained ground in Saxony. The University of Wittenberg made several alterations in the form of Church worship, abolishing, in particular, the celebration of private masses for the souls of the dead. Two events counteracted the pleasure of the reformer when the news came to him. He was told that the ancient University of Paris had condemned his doctrines, and that Henry VIII of England had written a reply to one of his books, so ably that the Pope had been delighted to confer on him the title of Defender of the Faith.

In 1522, Luther returned to Wittenberg, enjoying a harmless jest at Jena by the way. There his disguise of red mantle and doublet so deceived fellow-travellers that they told him their intention of going to see Martin Luther return, without realizing that they were speaking to the great reformer!

His next sermons were not fortunate in their results, since the peasants failed to understand them. A class war followed, in which Luther took the part of mediator, trying to show his poorer neighbours the evils their violence would bring on themselves, and reproaching the nobles with their oppressive customs. He was angry that the new religious spirit should be discredited by social disorder, and spoke bitterly of all who refused to heed his remonstrances. Erasmus was shocked by Luther's roughness of speech, and withdrew more and more from the reforming party. He hated the old monkish teaching and desired literary freedom, but he could not forgive the excesses of this thorough-going reformer.

In 1525, Luther gave grave offence to many of his own followers by marrying Catherine von Bora, a nun who had left her convent. He had cast off the Roman belief that a priest should never marry, but public feeling could not approve of a change which was in conflict with so many centuries of tradition. The Reformer's home life was happy, nevertheless, and six children were born of the marriage. As a father, Luther showed much tenderness. He wrote with a marvellous simplicity to his eldest son: "I know a very pretty, pleasant garden and in it there are a great many children, all dressed in little golden coats, picking up nice apples and pears and cherries and plums, under the trees. And they sing and jump about and are very merry; and besides, they have got beautiful little horses with golden bridles and silver saddles. Then I asked the man to whom the garden belonged, whose children they were, and he said, 'These are children who love to pray and learn their lessons, and do as they are bid'; then I said, 'Dear sir, I have a little son called Johnny Luther; may he come into this garden too?'"

Luther's translation of the Bible was read with wonderful attention by people of every rank. Other countries of Europe also were influenced by his doctrines, with the result of a diminution of the blind faith in priestcraft. Nuremburg, Frankfort, Hamburg, and other imperial free cities in Germany openly embraced the reformed religion, abolishing the mass and other "superstitious rites of popery." The secular princes drew up a list of one hundred grievances, enumerating the grievous burdens laid upon them by the Holy See. In 1526 a Diet assembled at Speyer to consider the state of religion! The Diet enjoined all those who had obeyed the decree issued against Luther at Worms to continue to observe it, and to prohibit other States from attempting any further innovation in religion till the meeting of a general council. The Elector of Saxony, with the heads of other principalities and free cities, entered a solemn "protest" against this decree, as unjust and impious. On that account they were distinguished by the name of Protestants.

At Augsburg, where priests and statesmen met together in 1530, the Protestant form of religion was established. The reformers issued there a "confession" of their faith, known as the Augsburg Confession, and which placed them for ever apart from the old Roman Catholic Church. A zeal for religion had seized on men excited by their own freedom to find the truth for themselves. Luther lamented the strife that of necessity followed, often wondering whether he had not been too bold in opposing the ancient traditions of Rome. For he had aimed at purification rather than separation, and would have preferred to keep the old Church rather than to set up a new one in its place. "He was never for throwing away old shoes till he had got new ones." Naturally reformers of less moderate nature did not love him. He detested argument for argument's sake. There was nothing crafty or subtle in his nature. He poured out the honest convictions of his heart without regard to the form in which he might express them.

In 1546, Luther had promised to settle a dispute between two nobles, and set out on his journey, feeling a presentiment that the end of worldly strife was come for him. On the way, he visited Eisleben, where he had been born, and there died. His body was taken to Wittenberg, the scene of his real life-work.

Germany had been restless before the reforms of Martin Luther, disinclined to believe all that was taught by monks and inculcated by tradition. The authority of the Pope had kept men's souls in bondage. They hardly dared to judge for themselves what was right and what was wrong. If money could free them from the burden of sins, they paid it gladly, acquitting themselves of all responsibility. Now conscience had stirred and the mind been slowly awakened. Luther declared his belief that each was responsible to God for his own soul, and there was a universal echo. " I *believe* in the forgiveness of sins." The truth which had shone on the troubled monk was the truth to abide for ever with his followers. " No priest can save you ! no masses or indulgences can help you ! But God has saved you ! " The voice of the preacher came to the weary, crying out from ancient cathedrals and passionately swaying the whole nation of Germany. Europe was in need of the same moral freedom. Other countries took up the new creed and examined it, finding that which would work like a leaven in the corruptness of the age.

Chapter VI

Charles V, Holy Roman Emperor

THE sixteenth century was an age of splendid monarchs, who vied with each other in the luxury of their courts, the chivalry of their bearing, and the extent of their possessions.

Francis I was a patron of the New Learning, the pride of France, ever devoted to a monarch with some dash of the heroic in his composition. He was dark and handsome, and excelled in the tournaments, where he tried to recapture the romance of the Middle Ages by his knightly equipment and gallant feats of arms.

Henry VIII, the King of England, was eager to spend the wealth he had inherited on the glittering pageants which made the people forget the tyranny of the Tudor monarchs. He was four years the senior of Francis, but still under thirty when Charles the Fifth succeeded, in 1516, to the wide realms of the Spanish Crown.

This king was likely to eclipse the pleasure-loving rivals of France and England, for he had vast power in Europe through inheritance of the great possessions of his house. Castile and Aragon came to Charles through his mother, Joanna, who was the daughter of Ferdinand and Isabella. Naples and Sicily went with Aragon, though, as a matter of fact, they had been appropriated in violation of a treaty. The Low Countries were part of the dominions of Charles' grandmother, Mary of

Burgundy, who had married Philip, the Archduke of Austria. When Maximilian of Austria died in 1519, he desired that his grandson should succeed not only to his dominions in Europe, but also to the proud title of Holy Roman Emperor, which was not hereditary. With the treasures of the New World at his disposal, through the discoveries of Christopher Columbus, Charles V had little doubt that he could obtain anything he coveted.

It was soon evident that Charles' claim to the Empire would be disputed by Francis I, who declared, " An he spent three millions of gold he would be Emperor." The French King had a fine army, and money enough to bribe the German princes, in whose hands the power of " electing " lay. Francis' ambassadors travelled from one to another with a train of horses, heavily laden with sumptuous offerings, but these found it quite impossible to bribe Frederick the Wise of Saxony.

Charles did not scruple to use bribery, and he hoped to win Henry of England by flattery and by appealing to him as a kinsman; for his aunt, Catherine of Aragon, was Henry's Queen at that time. The Tudor King had boldly taken for his motto, " Whom I defend is master," but he had secret designs on the Imperial throne himself, and thought either Francis I or Charles V would become far too powerful in Europe if the German electors appointed one of them.

The Pope entered into the struggle because he knew that Charles of Spain would be likely to destroy the peace of Italy by demanding the Duchy of Milan, which was then under French rule. He gave secret advice, therefore, to the German electors to choose one of their own number, and induced them to offer the Imperial rank to Frederick the Wise of Saxony.

Charles V Holy Roman Emperor

This prince did not feel strong enough to beat off the attacks of Selim, the ruler of the Ottoman Empire, then threatening the land of Hungary. He refused to become Emperor and suggested that the natural resistance to the East should come from Austria.

Charles, undoubtedly, had Spanish gold that would assist him in this struggle. In 1519 he was invested with the imperial crown and began to dream of further conquests. A quarrel with France followed, both sides having grievances that made friendship impossible at that period. Charles had offended Francis I by promising to aid d'Albert of Navarre to regain his kingdom. He also wished to claim the Duchy of Milan as the Pope had predicted, and was indignant that Burgundy, which had been filched from his grandmother by Louis XI, had never been restored to his family.

Francis renewed an ancient struggle in reclaiming Naples. He was determined not to yield to imperial pride, and sought every means of conciliating Henry VIII of England, who seemed eager to assert himself in Europe. The two monarchs met at the Field of the Cloth of Gold in 1513 and made a great display of friendship. They were both skilled horsemen and showed to advantage in a tournament, having youth and some pretensions to manly beauty in their favour. The meeting between them was costly and did not result as Francis had anticipated, since Charles V had been recently winning a new ally in the person of Cardinal Wolsey, the chief adviser of the young King of England.

Wolsey was ambitious and longed for the supreme honour of the Catholic Church. He believed that he might possibly attain this through the nephew of

Catherine of Aragon. He commended Charles to his master, and in the end gained for him an Austrian alliance. There was even some talk of a marriage between the Emperor and the little Princess Mary.

A treaty with the Pope made Charles V more sanguine of success than ever. Leo X belonged to the family of the Medici and hoped to restore the ancient prestige of that house. He was overjoyed to receive Parma and Placentia as a result of his friendship with the ambitious Emperor, and now agreed to the expulsion of the French from Milan on condition that Naples paid a higher tribute to the Papal See.

These arrangements were concluded without reference to Chièvres, the Flemish councillor, whose influence with Charles had once been paramount. Henceforward, the Emperor ruled his scattered empire, relying only upon his own strength and capability. He naturally met with disaffection among his subjects, for the Spaniards were jealous of his preference for the Netherlands, where he had been educated, and the people of Germany resented his long sojourn in Spain, thinking that they were thereby neglected. It would have been impossible for Charles to have led a more active life or to have striven more courageously to retain his hold over far distant countries. He was constantly travelling to the different parts of his empire, and made eleven sea-voyages during his reign—an admirable record in days when voyages were comparatively dangerous.

Charles changed his motto from *Nondum* to *Plus ultra* as he proceeded to send fleets across the ocean that the banner of Castile might float proudly on the distant shores of the Pacific. But the war with France was the real interest of the Emperor's life and he pursued it vigorously, obtaining supplies from the Spanish

Cortes or legislative authority of Spain. He gained the sympathy of that nation during his residence at Madrid from 1522-9 and pacified the rebellious spirit of the *Communes* which administered local affairs. His marriage with Isabella of Portugal proved, too, that he would maintain the traditions of the Spanish monarchy.

In 1521 the French were driven from the Duchy of Milan and in 1522 they were compelled to retire from Italy. In the following year the Constable of Bourbon deserted Francis to espouse the Emperor's cause, because he had received many insults from court favourites. He had been removed from the government of Milan, and was fond of quoting the words of an old Gascon knight first spoken in the reign of Charles VII : " Not three kingdoms like yours could make me forsake you, but one insult might."

Bourbon was rebuked for his faithlessness to his King at the battle of La Biagrasse where Bayard, that perfect knight, *sans peur et sans reproche*, fell with so many other French nobles. The Constable had compassion on the wounded man as he lay at the foot of a tree with his face still turned to the enemy. " Sir, you need have no pity for me," the knight answered bravely, " for I die an honest man ; but I have pity on you, seeing you serve against your prince, your country, and your oath."

Bourbon may have blushed at the rebuke, but he took the field gallantly at Pavia on behalf of the Emperor. Francis I had invaded Italy and occupied Milan, but he was not quick to follow up his success and met defeat at the hands of his vassal on February 24th, 1525, which was Charles V's twenty-fifth birthday. The flower of France fell on the battle-field, while the King himself was taken prisoner. He would not give up his sword to the traitor Bourbon, but continued to fight on foot after his horse had been shot under him. He proved that he was as punctilious a knight as Bayard, and wrote to his mother on the evening of this battle, "All is lost but honour."

The Emperor's army now had both France and Italy at their mercy. Bourbon decided to march on Rome, to the joy of his needy, avaricious soldiers. He took the ancient capital where the riches of centuries had accumulated; both Spaniards and Germans rioted on its treasures without restraint. They spared neither church nor palace, but defiled the most sacred places. The very ring was removed from the hand of Pope Julius as he lay within his tomb. Clement VII, the reigning Pope, was too feeble and vacillating to save himself, though it would have been quite possible. He was made a prisoner of war, for political motives inspired the Emperor to demand a heavy ransom.

The Ladies' Peace concluded the long war between Charles V and Francis I. It was so called because it was arranged through Louise, the French King's mother, and Margaret, the aunt who had taken charge of the Emperor in his childhood. These two ladies occupied adjoining houses in the town of Cambrai, and held consultations at any hour in the narrow passage between the two dwellings. The peace, finally drawn up in August 1529, was very shameful to Francis I, since he agreed to desert all his partisans in Italy and the Netherlands. He had purchased his own freedom by the treaty of Madrid in 1526.

In 1530, the Emperor, who had made a separate treaty with the Italian states, received the crown of Lombardy and crown of the Holy Roman Empire from the hands of the Pope at Bologna. On this occasion he was invested with a mantle studded with jewels and some ancient sandals. Ill-health and increasing melancholy clouded his delight in these honours. His aquiline features and dark colouring had formerly given him some claim to beauty, but now the heavy " Hapsburg " jaw began to show the settled obstinacy of a narrow nature. The iron crown of Italy weighed on him heavily, for he was stricken by remorse that he had disregarded the entreaties of the Pope for the rescue of the Knights of St John, whose settlement of Rhodes had been attacked by the Turkish infidels. He gave them Malta in order that he might appease his conscience. Religion claimed much of his attention after the long conflict with France was ended.

Heresy was spreading in Germany, where Luther gained a vast number of adherents. Charles issued an edict against the monk, but there was national resistance for him to face as a consequence. In 1530 he renewed the Edict of Worms and was opposed by a League of Protestant princes, who applied for help from England, France, and Denmark against the oppressive Emperor. He would have set himself to crush them if his dominions had not been menaced by Soliman the Magnificent, a Turkish Sultan with an immense army. He was obliged to secure the co-operation of the Protestants against the Turks that he might drive the latter from his eastern frontier.

Italians, Flemings, Hungarians, Bohemians, and Burgundians fought side by side with the German troops and drove the invader back to his own territory. When this danger was averted, France suddenly attacked Savoy, and the Emperor found that he must postpone his struggle with the Lutherans. A joint invasion of

France by Charles V and Henry VIII of England forced Francis to conclude humiliating peace at Crespy 1544. Three years later the death of the French King left his adversary free to crush the religious liberty of his German subjects.

The Emperor, who had declared himself on the side of the Papacy in 1521, now united with the Pope and Charles' brother Ferdinand, who had been given the government of all the Austrian lands. All three were determined to compel Germany to return to the old faith and the old subjection to the Empire. Their resolve seemed to be fulfilled when Maurice, Duke of Saxony, betrayed the Protestant cause, the allies of the German princes proved faithless, and the Elector of Saxony and the Landgrave of Hesse were taken prisoners at Mühlberg in April 1547.

The star of Austria was still in the ascendant, and Charles V could still quote his favourite phrase, "Myself and the lucky moment." He put Maurice in the place of the venerable Elector of Saxony, who had refused long ago to take a bribe, and let the Landgrave of Hesse lie in prison. He imagined that he had Germany at his feet, and exulted over the defenders of her freedom. There had been a faint hope in their hearts once that the Emperor would champion Luther's cause from political interest, but he did not need a weapon against the Pope since the Holy See was entirely subservient to his wishes. Bigotry, inherited from Spanish ancestors, showed itself in the Emperor now. In Spain and the Netherlands he used the terrible Inquisition to stamp out heresy. The Grand Inquisitors, who charged themselves with the religious welfare of these countries, claimed control over lay and clerical subjects in the name of their ruler.

Maurice was unscrupulous and intrigued with Henry II of France against the Emperor, who professed himself the Protector of the Princes of the Empire. A formidable army was raised, which took Charles at a disadvantage and drove him from Germany. The Peace of Augsburg, 1555, formally established Protestantism over a great part of the empire.

The Emperor felt uneasily that the star of the House of Austria was setting. After his failure to crush the heretics, he was troubled by ill-health and the gloomy spirit which he inherited from his mother Joanna. He was weary of travelling from one part of his dominions to another, and knew that he could never win more fame and riches than he had enjoyed. His son Philip was old enough to reign in his stead if he decided to cede the sovereignty. The old Roman Catholic faith drew him apart from the noise and strife of the world by its promise of rest and all the solaces of retirement.

In 1555 the Emperor held the solemn ceremony of abdication at Brussels, for he paid especial honour to his subjects of the Netherlands. He sat in a chair of state surrounded by a splendid retinue and recounted the famous deeds of his administration with a natural pride, dwelling on the hardships of constant journeying because he had been unwilling to trust the affairs of government to any other. Turning to Philip he bade him hold the laws of his country sacred and to maintain the Catholic faith in all its purity. As he spoke, all his hearers melted into tears, for the people of the Netherlands owed much gratitude to their ruler. And the ceremony which attended the transference of the Spanish crown to Philip was no less moving. Charles had chosen the monastery of San Yuste as his last dwelling on account of its warm, dry climate. After a tender farewell to his family he set out there in some state, many attendants going into retreat with him. Yuste was a pleasant peaceful village near the Spanish city of Plasencia. Deep silence brooded over it, and was only broken by the bells of the convent the Emperor was entering. He found that a building had been erected for his " palace " in a garden planted with orange trees and myrtles. This was sumptuously furnished according to the monks' ideas, for Charles did not intend to adopt the simplicity of these brothers of St Jerome. Velvet canopies, rich tapestries, and Turkey carpets had been brought for the rooms which were prepared for a royal inmate. The walls of the Emperor's bedchamber were hung in black in token of his deep mourning for his mother, but many pictures from the brush of Titian were hung in that apartment. As Charles lay in bed he could see the famous " Gloria," which represented the emperor and empress of a bygone age in the midst of a throng of angels. He could also join in the chants of the monks without rising, if he were suffering from gout, for a window opened directly from his room into the chapel of the monastery. Sixty attendants were still in the service of the recluse, and those in the culinary office found it hard to satisfy the appetite of a monarch who, if he had given up his throne, had not by any means renounced the pleasures of the table.

A Keeper of the Wardrobe had been brought to Yuste, although Charles was plain in his attire and had somewhat disdained the personal vanity of his great rivals. He was parsimonious in such matters and hated to see good clothes spoilt, as he showed when he removed a new velvet cap in a sudden storm and sent to his palace for an old one! He observed fast-days, though he did not dine with the monks, and he lived the regular life of the monastery. The monks grew restive under the constant supervision which he exercised, and one of them is said to have remonstrated with the royal inmate, saying, " Cannot you be contented with having so long turned the world upside down, without coming here to disturb the quiet of a convent ? "

Charles amused many hours of leisure by mechanical employments in which he was assisted by one Torriano, who constructed a sundial in the convent-garden. He had a great fancy for clocks, and had a number of these in his royal apartments. The special triumphs of Torriano were some tin soldiers, so constructed that they could go through military exercises, and little wooden birds which flew in and out of the window and excited the admiring wonder of the monks walking in the convent garden.

Many visitors were received by the Emperor in his retirement. He still took an interest in the events of Europe, and received with the deepest sorrow the news that Calais had been lost by Philip's English wife. He was always ready to give his successor advice, and became more and more intolerant in religious questions. " Tell the Grand Inquisitor from me," he wrote, " to be at his post and lay the axe to the root of the tree before it spreads further. I rely on your zeal for bringing the guilty to punishment and for having them punished without favour to anyone, with all the severity which their crimes demand." After this impressive exhortation to Philip, he added a codicil to his will, conjuring him earnestly to bring to justice every heretic in his dominions.

Chapter VII

The Beggars of the Sea

THE Netherlands, lying like a kind of debateable land between France and Germany, were apt to be influenced by the different forms of Protestantism which were established in those countries. The inhabitants were remarkably quick-witted and attracted by anything which appealed to their reason. Their breadth of mind and cosmopolitan outlook was, no doubt, largely due to the extensive trade they carried on with eastern and western nations. The citizens of the well-built towns studding the Low Countries, had become very wealthy. They could send out fine soldiers, as Charles V had seen, but their chief pursuit was commerce. Education rendered them far superior to many other Europeans, who were scarcely delivered from the ignorance and superstition of the Middle Ages. Having proved themselves strong enough to be independent, they formed a Confederacy of Republics on the death of Charles V in 1558.

The Emperor was sincerely mourned because he had possessed Flemish tastes, yet he had always failed in his attempts to unite the whole of the Low Countries into one kingdom. There were no less than seventeen provinces in the Netherlands, with seventeen petty princes over them. Each province disdained the other as quite alien and foreign. Both French and a dialect of German were spoken by the natives. It was a great drawback to Philip II, their new ruler, that he could only speak Castilian.

Philip had been unpopular from the time of his first visit to the Netherlands, before the French war was settled by the treaty of Cateau Cambrésis. The credit of the settlement was chiefly due to the subtle diplomacy of William, Prince of Orange, the trusted councillor of Charles V, on whose shoulder the Emperor leant during the ceremony of abdication.

William of Orange yielded to none in pride of birth, being descended from one of the most illustrious houses of the Low Countries. He was young, gallant, and fond of splendour when he negotiated on the Emperor's behalf with Henry II of France. He managed matters so successfully that the Emperor was able to withdraw without loss of prestige from a war he was anxious to end at any cost. William received his nickname of the Silent during his residence as a hostage at the French court.

One day, at a hunting party, Henry II uncautiously told Orange of a plan he had made with Philip to stamp out every heretic in their dominions of France and the Netherlands by a sudden deadly onslaught that would allow the Protestants no time for resistance. It was assumed that William, being a powerful Catholic noble, would rejoice in this scheme. He held his peace very wisely but, in reality, he was full of indignation. He cared nothing for the reformed religion in itself, but he was a humane generous man, and from that hour determined that he would defend the helpless, persecuted Protestants of the Low Countries.

Philip II was not long in showing himself zealous to observe his father's instructions to preserve the Catholic faith in all its purity. He renewed the edict or " placard" against heresy which had been first issued in 1550. This provided for the punishment of anyone who should " print, write, copy, keep, conceal, sell, buy, or give in churches, streets, or other places " any book of the Reformers, anyone who should hold conventicles, or anyone who should converse or dispute concerning the Holy Scriptures, to say nothing of those venturing to entertain the opinions of heretics. The men were to be executed with the sword and the women buried alive, if they should persist in their errors. If they were firm in holding to their beliefs, such deaths were held too merciful. Execution by fire was a punishment that was universal in the days of the Spanish Inquisition.

Philip watched the burning of his heretic subjects with apparent satisfaction. The first ceremony that greeted him on his return to Spain was an *Auto da fé*, or Act of Faith, in which many victims were led to the stake. The scene was the great square of Valladolid in front of the Church of Saint Francis, and the hour of six was the signal for the bells to toll which brought forth that dismal train from the fortress of the Inquisition. Troops marched before the hapless men and women, who were clad in the hideous garb known as the *San Benito*—a loose sack of yellow cloth which was embroidered with figures of flames and devils feeding on them, in token of the destiny that would attend the heretics, soul and body. A pasteboard cap bore similar devices, and added grotesque pathos to the suffering faces of the martyrs. Judges and magistrates followed them, and nobles of the land were there on horseback, while members of the dread tribunal came after these, bearing aloft the arms of the Inquisition.

Philip occupied a seat upon the platform erected

Philip II present at an Auto-da-Fé
D. Valdivieso

opposite to the scaffold. It was his duty to draw his sword from the scabbard and to repeat an oath that he would maintain the purity of the Catholic faith before he witnessed the execution of "the enemies of God," as he thought all those who laid down their lives for the sake of heretical scruples.

A few who recanted were pardoned, but for the majority recantation only meant long imprisonment in cells where many hearts broke after years of solitude. The property of the accused was confiscated in any case; and this rule was a sore temptation to informers, who received a certain share of their neighbour's goods if they denounced him. When the "reconciled" had been sent back to prison under a strong guard, all eyes were fixed on the unrepentant. These wore cards round their necks and carried in their hands either a cross, or an inverted torch, which was a sign that their own life would shortly be extinguished. Few of these showed weakness, since they had already triumphed over long-protracted torture. They walked with head erect to the *quemada* or place of execution.

Dominican monks, by whose fanatic zeal the Holy Office gained a hold on every Spaniard, often walked among the doomed, stripped of their former vestments. Once a noble Florentine appealed to Philip as he was led by the royal gallery. "Is it thus that you allow your innocent subjects to be persecuted?" The King's face hardened, and his reply came sharply. "If it were my own son, I would fetch the wood to burn him, were he such a wretch as thou art." And there is no doubt that Philip spoke truth when he uttered words so merciless.

Under the royal sanction the persecution was continued in the Netherlands. It had closed the domains of science and speculation for Spain. It must break the free republican spirit of the Low Countries. Charles V had been afraid of injuring the trade which enabled him to pay a vast, all-conquering army. His son was less tolerant, and thought religion of greater importance even than military successes.

The terror of that formidable band of Inquisitors came upon the Protestant Flemings like the shadow on some sunny hill-side. They had lived in comfort and independence, resisting every attempt at royal tyranny. Now a worse tyranny was ruling in their midst—secret, relentless, inhuman—demanding toll of lives for sacrifice. Philip was zealous in appointing new bishops, each of whom should have inquisitors to aid in the work of hunting down the Protestants. "There are but few of us left in the world who care for religion," he wrote, " 'tis necessary therefore for us to take the greater need for Christianity."

Granvelle, a cardinal of the Catholic Church, was the ruler of the Low Countries, terrorizing Margaret of Parma, whom Philip had appointed to act there as his Regent. Margaret was a worthy woman of masculine tastes and habits; she was the daughter of Charles V and therefore a half-sister of Philip. She would have won some concessions for the Protestants, knowing the temper of the Flemish, to whom she was allied by birth, but Granvelle was artful in his policy and managed by frequent correspondence with Spain to baffle the efforts of the whole party, which looked with indignation on the work of the Inquisitors. Peter Titelmann, the chief instrument of the Holy Office in the Netherlands, alarmed Margaret as well as her subjects, who were at the mercy of this monster. He rode through the country on horseback, dragging suspected persons from their very beds, and glorying in the knowledge that none dared resist him. He burst into a house at Ryssel one day, seized John de Swarte, his wife and four children, together with two newly-married couples and two other persons, convicted them of reading the Bible, of praying within their own dwellings, and had them all immediately burned. No wonder that the Duchess of Parma trembled when the same man clamoured at the doors of her chamber for admittance. High and low were equally in danger. Even the royal family were at the mercy of the Holy Office. Spies might be found in any household, and both men and women disappeared to answer "inquiries" made with torture of the rack, without knowing their accusers.

Granvelle had enemies, who bent themselves to accomplish the downfall of the minister. He was of humble origin, though he had amassed great wealth and possessed a remarkable capacity for administration. Egmont, the fierce, quarrelsome soldier, was his chief adversary among the nobles. There was a lively scene when Egmont drew his sword on the Cardinal in the presence of the Regent.

William of Orange was, perhaps, the one man whom all respected for his true courage and strength of character. Granvelle wrote of him to Philip as highly dangerous, knowing that in the Silent he had met his match in cunning; for William's qualities were strangely mingled—he had vast ambition and yet took up a cause later that broke his splendid fortunes. He was upright, yet he had few scruples in dealing with opponents. He would employ spies to acquaint him with secret papers and use every possible means of gaining an advantage.

Egmont and Orange vied with each other in the state they kept, their wives being bitterly jealous of each other. William's second marriage had been arranged for worldly motives. His bride was Princess Anna of Saxony, daughter of the Elector Maurice who had worked such evil for the Emperor Charles and had embraced the new religion. The Princess was only sixteen; she limped, and was by no means handsome. It was hinted, too, that her temper was stormy and her mind narrow. The advantages of the match consisted in her high rank, which was above that of Orange. Philip disliked the wedding of a Reformer with one of his most powerful subjects. He disliked the bride's family, as was natural, and the bride's family did not approve of her wedding with a " Papist." The ceremony took place on St Bartholomew's Day, 1561.

After his second marriage the Prince of Orange continued to exercise a lordly hospitality, for his staff of cooks was famous. His wife quarrelled for precedence with the Countess Egmont, till the two were obliged to walk about the streets arm-in-arm because neither would acknowledge an inferior station. Being magnificently dressed, they suffered much inconvenience from narrow doorways, which were not built to admit more than one dame in the costume of the period. The times were not yet too serious to forbid such petty bickering, and there was a certain section of society quite frivolous enough to enjoy the ridiculous side of it.

Margaret of Parma openly showed her delight when Granvelle was banished, for she felt herself relieved from a tyrant. She now gave her confidence to Orange, who was very popular with the people. There seemed to be some hope of inducing Philip to withdraw some of the edicts against his Protestant subjects. Their cries were daily becoming louder, and there was an uneasy spirit abroad in the Low Countries which greeted with delight the device of Count Egmont for a new livery for his servants that should condemn the ostentation of such ministers as Granvelle. His retainers appeared in doublet and hose of the coarsest grey material, with long hanging sleeves and no embroideries. They wore an emblem of a fool's cap and bells, or a monk's cowl, which was supposed to mock the Cardinal's contemptuous allusion to the nobles as buffoons. The King was furious at the fashion which soon spread among the courtiers. They changed the device then to a bundle of arrows or a wheat-sheaf which, they asserted, denoted the union of all their hearts in the King's service. Schoolboys could not have betrayed more joy in the absence of their pedagogue than the whole court showed when Granvelle left the country in 1564 on a pretended visit to his mother.

Orange had now three aims in life, to convoke the States-General, to moderate or abolish the edicts, and to suppress both council of finance and privy council, leaving only the one council of state, which he could make the body of reform. By this time the persecutions were rousing the horror of Catholic as well as Calvinist. The prisons were crowded with victims, and through the streets went continual processions to the stake. The four estates of Flanders were united in an appeal to Philip. Egmont was to visit Spain and point out the uselessness of forcing the Netherlands to accept religious decrees which reduced them to abject slavery. Before he set out, William of Orange made a notable speech, declaring the provinces free and determined to vindicate their freedom.

Egmont's visit was a failure, since he suffered himself to be won by the flattery of Philip II. He was reproached with having forgotten the interests of the State when he returned, and was consumed by regrets that were unavailing. The wrath of the people was increasing daily as the cruel persecution devastated the Low Countries. All other subjects were forgotten in the time of agony and expectation. There was talk of resistance that would win death on the battlefield, more merciful than that proceeding from slow torture. In streets, shops, and taverns men gathered to whisper of the dark deeds done in the name of the Inquisition. Philip had vowed " never to allow myself either to become or to be called the lord of those who reject Thee for their Lord," as he prostrated his body before a crucifix. The doom of the Protestants had been sealed by that oath. Henceforth, those who feared death were known to favour freedom of religion.

The Duke of Alva was firm in his support of Philip's measures. The Inquisition was formally proclaimed in the market-place of every town and village in the Netherlands. Resistance was certain. All knew that contending armies would take the field soon. Commerce ceased to engage the attention of the people. Those merchants and artisans who were able left the cities. Patriots spoke what was in their hearts at last, and pamphlets " snowed in the streets." The " League of the Compromise " was formed in 1566, with Count Louis of Nassau as the leader; it declared the Inquisition " iniquitous, contrary to all laws, human and divine, surpassing the greatest barbarism which was ever practised by tyrants, and as redounding to the dishonour of God and to the total desolation of the country." The members of the League might be good Catholics though they were pledged to resist the Inquisition. They always promised to attempt nothing " to the diminution of the King's grandeur, majesty, or dominion."

All who signed the Compromise were to be mutually protected by an oath which permitted none to be persecuted. It was a League, in fact, against the foreign government of the Netherlands, signed by nobles whose spirit was roused to protest against the influence of such men as Alva.

The Compromise did not gain the support of William of Orange because he was distrustful of its objects. The members were young and imprudent, and many of them were not at all disinterested in their desire to secure the broad lands belonging to the Catholic Church. Their wild banquets were dangerous to the whole country, since spies sat at the board and took note of all extravagant phrases that might be construed into disloyalty. Orange himself held meetings of a very different sort in his sincere endeavour to avert the catastrophe he feared.

Troops rode into Brussels, avowing their intention to free the country from Spanish tyranny. Brederode was among them—a handsome reckless noble, descended from one of the oldest families of Holland. The citizens welcomed the soldiers with applause and betrayed the same enthusiasm on the following day when a procession of noble cavaliers went to present a petition to Margaret of Parma, urging that she should suspend the powers of the Inquisition while a messenger was sent to Spain to demand its abolition.

As the petitioners left the hall, they heard with furious resentment the remark of one Berlaymont to the troubled Regent. "What, Madam! is it possible that your highness can entertain fears of these beggars? (*gueux*). Is it not obvious what manner of men they are? They have not had wisdom enough to manage their own estates, and are they now to teach the King and Your Highness how to govern the country? By the living God, if my advice were taken, their petition should have a cudgel for a commentary, and we would make them go down the steps of the palace a great deal faster than they mounted them."

The Confederates received an answer from the Duchess not altogether to their satisfaction, though she promised to make a special application to the King for the modification of edicts and ordered the Inquisitors to proceed " moderately and discreetly " with their office. Three hundred guests met at Brederode's banquet on the 8th of April, and there and then, amid the noise of revelry and the clink of wine-cups, they adopted the name of " Beggars," flung at them in scorn by Berlaymont.

Brederode was the first to call for a wallet, which he hung round his neck after the manner of those who begged their bread. He filled a large wooden bowl as part of his equipment, lifted it with both hands and drained it, crying, " Long live the Beggars! " The cry was taken up as each guest donned the wallet in turn and drank from the bowl to the Beggars' health. The symbols of the brotherhood were hung up in the hall so that all might stand underneath to repeat certain words as he flung salt into a goblet:

> " By this salt, by this head, by this wallet still,
> These beggars change not, fret who will."

A costume was adopted in accordance with the fantastic humour of the nobles. Soon Brussels stared at quaint figures in coarse grey garments, wearing felt hats, and carrying the beggar's bowl and wallet. The badges which adorned their hats protested fidelity to Philip.

The Beggars of the Sea

Twelve of the Beggars sought an interview with the Duchess of Parma to demand that Orange, Egmont, and Admiral Hoorn should be appointed to guard the interests of the States, and they even threatened to form foreign alliances if Margaret refused to grant what they wanted. They knew that they could count now on assistance from the Hugenot leaders in France and from the Protestant princes in Germany.

The war was imminent in which the Beggars would avenge the insult uttered by the haughty lips of Berlaymont. The sea-power of Holland had its origin in the first fleet which the Sea-Beggars equipped in 1569. These corsairs who cruised in the narrow waters and descended upon the seaport towns were of many different nationalities, but were one and all inspired by a fanatic hatred of the Spaniard and the Papist.

Chapter VIII

William the Silent, Father of his Country

THE confusion which reigned in the Netherlands sorely troubled Margaret of Parma, who wrote to Philip for men and money that she might put down the rising. She received nothing beyond vague promises that he would come one day to visit his dominions overseas. It was still the belief of the King of Spain that he held supreme authority in a country where many a Flemish noble claimed a higher rank, declaring that the so-called sovereign was only Duke of Brabant and Count of Flanders.

In despair, the Regent called on Orange, Hoorn, and Egmont to help her in restoring order. Refugees had come back from foreign countries and were holding religious services openly, troops of Protestants marched about the streets singing Psalms and shouting " Long live the Beggars ! " It seemed to Margaret of Parma, a devout Catholic, that for the people there was " neither faith nor King."

William, as Burgrave of Antwerp, was able to restore order in that city, promising the citizens that they should have the right to assemble for worship outside the walls. A change had come over this once worldly noble—henceforth he cared nothing for the pomps and vanities of life. He had decided to devote himself to the cause of the persecuted, however dear it cost him.

The Prince of Orange hoped that Egmont would join him in resistance to the Spanish tyranny. Egmont was beloved by the people of the Netherlands as a soldier who had proved his valour; his high rank and proud nature might have been expected to make him resentful of authority that would place him in subjection. But William parted from his friend, recognizing sadly that they were inspired by different motives. "Alas! Egmont," he said, embracing the noble who would not desert the cause of Philip, "the King's clemency, of which you boast, will destroy you. Would that I might be deceived, but I foresee too clearly that you are to be the bridge which the Spaniards will destroy so soon as they have passed over it to invade our country."

William found himself soon in a state of isolation. He refused to take a new oath of fidelity to the King, which bound him to "act for or against whomsoever his Majesty might order without restriction or limitation." His own wife was a Lutheran, and by such a promise it might become his duty to destroy her! An alliance with foreign princes was the only safeguard against the force which Spain was preparing. The Elector of Saxony was willing to enter into a League to defend the reformed faith of the Netherlands. Meantime, after resigning all his offices, the Prince of Orange went into exile with his entire household.

In 1567 Philip ceased his vacillation. He sent the Duke of Alva to stamp out heresy at any cost in the Low Countries.

Alva was the foremost general of his time, a soldier whose life had been one long campaign in Europe. He had a kind of fierce fanatical religion which led him to revenge his father's death at the hands of the Moors on many a hapless Christian. He was avaricious, and the lust for booty determined him to sack the rich cities of the Netherlands without regard for honour. He was in his sixtieth year, but time had not weakened his strong inflexible courage. Tall, thin, and erect, he carried himself as a Spaniard of noble blood, and yielded to none in the superb arrogance of his manners. His long beard gave him the dignity of age, and his bearing stamped him always as a conqueror who knew nothing of compassion. It was hopeless to appeal to the humanity of Toledo, Duke of Alva. A stern disciplinarian, he could control his troops better than any general Philip had, yet he did not wish to check their excesses, and seemed to look with pleasure upon the awful scenes of a war in which no quarter was given.

Alva led a picked army of 10,000 men—Italian foot soldiers for the most part, with some musketeers among them—who would astonish the simple northern people he held in such contempt. "I have trained people of iron in my day," was his boast. "Shall I not easily crush these people of butter?"

At first the people of the Netherlands seemed likely to be cowed into complete submission. Egmont came out to meet Alva, bringing him two beautiful horses as a present. The Spaniard had already doomed this man to the block, but he pretended great pleasure at the welcome gift and put his arms round the neck which he knew would not rest long on Egmont's shoulders. He spoke very graciously to the escort who led him into Brussels.

Margaret of Parma was still Regent in name, but in reality she had been superseded by the Captain-General of the Spanish forces. She was furious at the slight, and showed her displeasure by greeting the Duke of Alva coldly. After writing to Philip to expostulate, she discovered that her position would not be restored, and therefore retired to Parma.

Egmont and Hoorn were the first victims of Alva's treachery. They died on the same day, displaying such fortitude at the last that the people mourned them passionately, and a storm of indignation burst forth against Philip II and the agent he had sent to shed the noblest blood of the Low Countries.

Alva set up a " Council of Troubles " so that he could dispatch other victims with the same celerity. This became known as " the Council of Blood " from the merciless nature of its transactions. Anyone who chose to give evidence against his friends was assured that he would have a generous reward for such betrayals. The Duke of Alva was President of the Council and had the right of final decision in all cases. Few were saved from the sword or the stake, since by blood alone the rebel and the heretic were to be crushed and Philip's sovereignty established firmly in the Netherlands.

In 1568 William of Orange was ordered to appear before the court and, on his refusal, was declared an outlaw. His eldest son was captured at the University of Louvain and sent to the Spanish court that he might unlearn the principles in which he had been educated.

Orange issued a justification of his conduct, but even this was held to be an act of defiance against the authority of Philip. The once loyal subject determined to expel the King's troops from the Low Countries, believing himself chosen by God to save the reformers from the pitiless oppression of the Spanish. He had already changed his views on religion. Prudence seemed to have forsaken the astute Prince of Orange. He proceeded to raise an army, though he had not enough money to pay his mercenaries. He was preparing for a struggle against a general, second to none in Europe, a general, moreover, who had veterans at his command and the authority of Spain behind him. Yet the first disaster did not daunt either William of Orange or his brother Louis of Nassau, who was also a chivalrous leader of the people. " With God's help I am determined to go on," were the words inspired by Alva's triumph. There were Reformers in other countries ready to send help to their brethren in religion. Elizabeth of England had extended a welcome to thousands of Flemish traders. It was William's constant hope that she would send a force openly to his assistance.

Elizabeth, however, did not like rebels and was not minded to show sympathy with the enemies of Philip, who kept his troops from an attack on England. She would secretly encourage the Beggars to take Spanish ships, but she would not send an army of sufficient strength to ensure a decisive victory for the Reformers of the Netherlands.

Alva exulted in the loss of prestige which attended his enemy's flight from the Huguenot camp in the garb of a German peasant. He regarded William as a dead man, since he was driven to wander about the country, suffering from the condemnation of his allies because he had not been successful. Alva's victory would have seemed too easy if there had not been a terrible lack of funds among the Spanish, owing to the plunder which was carried off from Spain by Elizabethan seamen. The Spanish general demanded taxes suddenly

Last Moments of Count Egmont
Louis Gallait

from the people of the Netherlands, and expected that they would be paid without a murmur.

But he had mistaken the spirit of a trading country which was not subservient in its loyalty to any ruler. These prosperous merchants had always been accustomed to dispose of the money they earned according to their own wishes. Enemies of the Spanish sprang up among their former allies. Catholics as well as Protestants were angry at Alva's demand of a tax of the " hundredth penny " to be levied on all property. Alva's name had been detested even before he marched into the Low Countries with the army which was notorious for deeds of blood and outrage. Now it roused such violent hatred that men who had been ready to support his measures for their own interests gradually forsook him.

In July 1570, an amnesty was declared by the Duke of Alva in the great square of Antwerp. Philip's approaching marriage with Anne of Austria ought to have been celebrated with some appearance of goodwill to all men, but it was at this time that the blackest treachery stained Philip's name, already associated with stern cruelty.

Montigny, the son of the Dowager Countess of Hoorn, was one of the envoys sent to Philip's court before the war had actually opened. He had been detained in Spain and feared death, for he was a prisoner in the castle of Segovia. Philip had intended from the beginning to destroy Montigny, but he did not choose to order his execution openly. The knight had been sentenced by the Council of Blood after three years imprisonment, but still lingered on, hoping for release through the exertions of his family. The King was busied with wedding preparations, but not too busy to carry out a crafty scheme by which Montigny seemed to have died of fever, whereas he was strangled in the Castle. The hypocrisy of the Spanish monarch was so complete that he actually ordered suits of mourning for Montigny's servants.

In 1572 the Beggars, always restlessly cruising against their foes on the high seas, took Brill in the absence of a Spanish garrison. Their action was so successful that they hoisted the rebel flag over the little fort and took an oath with the inhabitants to acknowledge the Prince of Orange as their Stadtholder. Brill was an unexpected triumph which the brilliant, impetuous Louis of Nassau followed up by the seizure of Flushing, the key of Zealand, which was the approach to Antwerp. The Sea-Beggars then swarmed over the whole of Walcheren, receiving many recruits in their ranks and pillaging churches recklessly. Middelburg alone remained to the Spanish troops, while the provinces of the North began to look to the Prince of Orange as their legitimate ruler.

William looked askance at the disorderly feats of the Beggars, but the capture of important towns inspired him to fresh efforts. He corresponded with many foreign countries and had his agents everywhere. Sainte Aldgonde was one of the prime movers in these negotiations. He was a poet as well as a soldier, and wrote the stirring national anthem of *Wilhelmus van Nassouwen*, which is still sung in the Netherlands. Burghers now opened their purses to give money, for they felt that victories must surely follow the capture of Brill and Flushing. William took the field with hired soldiers, and was met by the news of the terrible massacre of Protestants in France in 1572 on the Eve of St Bartholomew. All his hopes of help from France were dashed to the ground at once, and for the moment he was daunted. Louis of Nassau was besieged at Mons by Alva. He tried to relieve his brother, but was ignominiously prevented by the *Camisaders* who made their way to his camp at night, wearing white shirts over their armour, and killed eight hundred of his soldiers.

William threw in his lot, once for all, with the Northern provinces, receiving a hearty welcome from Holland and Zealand, states both maintaining a gallant struggle. He was recognized as Stadtholder by a meeting of the States in 1572, and liberty of worship was established for Protestants and Catholics. His authority was absolute in this region of the Low Countries.

Alva revenged himself for the resistance of Mons by the brutal sack of Malines and of Zutphen. The outrages of his soldiers were almost inhuman, and immense booty was captured, to the satisfaction of the leader.

Amsterdam was loyal to Philip, but Haarlem was in the hands of Calvinists. The Spanish army advanced on this town expecting to take it at the first assault, but they met with a stubborn resistance. The citizens had in their minds the horror of the sack of Zutphen. They repulsed one assault after another and the siege, begun in December 1572, was turned into a blockade, and still the Spaniards could not enter. The heads of the leaders of relief armies which had been defeated were flung into Haarlem with insulting gibes. The reply to this was a barrel which was sent rolling out carrying eleven heads, ten in payment of the tax of one-tenth hitherto refused to Alva and the eleventh as interest on the sum which had not been paid quite promptly! It was in July 1573, when the citizens had been reduced by famine to the consumption of weeds, shoe-leather, and vermin, that the Spanish army entered Haarlem.

The loss on both sides was enormous, and William had reason to despair. Only 1600 were left of a garrison of 4000. It seemed as if the courage of Haarlem had been unavailing, for gibbets rose on all sides to exhibit the leaders of the desperate resistance.

But the fleets of the Beggars rode the sea in triumph, and the example of Haarlem had given spirit to other towns unwilling to be beaten in endurance. Alva was disappointed to find that immediate submission did not follow. He left the country in 1573, declaring that his health and strength were gone, and he was unwilling to lose his reputation.

Don Luis Requesens, his successor, would have made terms, but William of Orange adhered to certain resolutions. There must be freedom of worship throughout the Netherlands, where all the ancient charters of liberty must be restored and every Spaniard must resign his office. William then declared himself a Calvinist, probably for patriotic reasons.

The hope of assistance from France and England rose again inevitably. Louis of Nassau obtained a large sum of French money and intended to raise troops for the relief of Leyden, which was invested by the Spaniards in 1574. He gathered a force of mixed nationality and no cohesion, and was surprised and killed with his gallant brother Henry. Their loss was a great blow to William, who felt that the responsibilities of the war henceforward rested solely on his shoulders.

Leyden was relieved by the desperate device of cutting the dykes and opening the sluices to flood the land around it. A fleet was thus enabled to sail in amidst fields and farmhouses to attack the besieging

Spanish. The Sea-Beggars were driven by the wind to the outskirts of Leyden, where they engaged in mortal conflict. The forts fell into their hands, some being deserted by the Spanish who fled from the rising waters. William of Orange received the news at Delft, where he had taken up his residence. He founded the University of Leyden as a memorial of the citizens' endurance. The victory, however, was modified some months later by the capture of Zierickzee, which gave the Spaniards an outlet on the sea and also cut off Walcheren from Holland.

In sheer desperation William made overtures to Queen Elizabeth, offering her the sovereignty of Holland and Zealand if she would engage in the struggle against Spain. Elizabeth dared not refuse, lest France should step into the breach, but she was unwilling to declare herself publicly on the side of rebels.

In April 1576 an Act of Federation was signed which formally united the two States of Zealand and Holland and conferred the supreme authority on the Prince of Orange, commander in war and governor in peace. Requesens was dead; a general patriotic rising was imminent. On September 26th the States-General met at Brussels to discuss the question of uniting all the provinces.

The Spanish Fury at Antwerp caused general consternation in the Netherlands. The ancient town was attacked quite suddenly, all its wealth falling into the hands of rapacious soldiers. No less than 7000 citizens met their death at the hands of men who carried the standard of Christ on the Cross and knelt to ask God's blessing before they entered on the massacre! Greed for gold had come upon the Spaniards, who hastened to secure the treasures accumulated at Antwerp. Jewels and velvets and laces were coveted as much as the contents of the strong boxes of the merchants, and torture was employed to discover the plate and money that were hidden. A wedding-party was interrupted, and the clothes of the bride stripped from her. Many palaces fell by fire and the splendid Town House perished. For two whole days the city was the scene of indescribable horrors.

The Pacification of Ghent had been signed when the news of the Spanish Fury reached the States-General. The members of this united with the Prince of Orange, as ruler of Holland and Zealand, to drive the foreigner from their country. The Union of Brussels confirmed this treaty in January 1577, for the South were anxious to rid themselves of the Spaniards though they desired to maintain the Catholic religion. Don John of Austria, Philip II's half-brother, was accepted as Governor-General after he had given a general promise to observe the wishes of the people.

Don John made a state entry into Brussels, but he soon found that the Prince of Orange had gained complete ascendancy over the Netherlands and that he was by no means free to govern as he chose. Don John soon grew weary of a position of dependence; he seized Namur and took up his residence there, afterwards defying the States-General. A universal cry for Orange was raised in the confusion that followed, and William returned in triumph to the palace of Nassau. Both North and South demanded that he should be their leader; both Protestant and Catholic promised to regard his government as legal.

In January 1578, the Archduke Matthias, brother of the Emperor, was invited by the Catholic party to enter Brussels as its governor. William welcomed

William the Silent

the intruder, knowing that the supreme power was still vested in himself, but he was dismayed to see Alexander of Parma join Don John, realizing that their combined armies would be more than a match for his. Confusion returned after a victory of Parma, who was an able and brilliant general. The Catholic Duke of Anjou took Mons, and John Casimir, brother of the Elector-Palatine, entered the Netherlands from the east as the champion of the extreme Calvinists.

The old religious antagonism was destroying the union of the provinces. William made immense exertions and succeeded in securing the alliance of Queen Elizabeth, Henry of Navarre, and John Casimir, while the Duke of Anjou accepted the title of Defender of the Liberties of the Netherlands. His work seemed undone on the death of Don John in 1578 and the succession of Alexander, Duke of Parma. This Prince sowed the seeds of discord very skilfully, separating the Walloon provinces from the Reformers. A party of Catholic Malcontents was formed in protest against the excesses of the Calvinists. Religious tolerance was to be found nowhere, save in the heart of William of Orange. North and South separated in January 1579, and made treaties which bound them respectively to protect their own form of religion.

Attempts were made to induce Orange to leave the Netherlands that Spain might recover her lost sovereignty. He was surrounded by foes, and many plots were formed against him. In March 1581, King Philip denounced him as the enemy of the human race, a traitor and a miscreant, and offered a heavy bribe to anyone who would take the life of " this pest " or deliver him dead or alive.

William's defence, known to the authorities as his

Apology, was issued in every court of Europe. In it he dwelt on the different actions of his long career, and pointed out Philip's crimes and misdemeanours. His own Imperial descent was contrasted with the King of Spain's less illustrious ancestry, and an eloquent appeal to the people for whom he had made heroic sacrifices was signed by the motto *Je le maintiendrai*. ("I will maintain.")

The Duke of Anjou accepted the proffered sovereignty of the United Netherlands in September 1580, but Holland and Zealand refused to acknowledge any other ruler than William of Orange, who received the title of Count, and joined with the other States in casting off their allegiance to Philip. The French Prince was invested with the ducal mantle by Orange when he entered Antwerp as Duke of Brabant, and was, in reality, subject to the idol of the Netherlands. The French protectorate came to an end with the disgraceful scenes of the French Fury, when the Duke's followers attempted to seize the chief towns, crying at Antwerp, "Long live the Mass! Long live the Duke of Anjou! Kill! Kill!"

Orange would still have held to the French in preference to the Spanish, but the people did not share his views, and were suspicious of his motives when he married a daughter of that famous Huguenot leader, Admiral de Coligny.

Orange retired to Delft, sorely troubled by the distrust of the nation, and the Catholic nobles were gradually lured back by Parma to the Spanish party. In 1584 a young Burgundian managed to elude the vigilance of William's retainers; he made his way into the *Prinsenhof* and fired at the Prince as he came from dinner with his family.

The Prince of Orange fell, crying "My God, have pity on my soul and on this poor people." He had now forfeited his life as well as his worldly fortunes, but the struggle he had waged for nearly twenty years had a truly glorious ending. The genius of one man had given freedom to the far-famed Dutch Republic, founded on the States acknowledging William their Father.

Chapter IX

Henry of Navarre

THROUGHOUT France the followers of John Calvin of Geneva organized themselves into a powerful Protestant party. The Reformation in Germany had been aristocratic in tendency, since it was mainly upheld by princes whose politics led them to oppose the Papacy. The teaching of Calvin appealed more directly to the ignorant, for his creed was stern and simple. The Calvinists even declared Luther an agent of the devil, in striking contrast to their own leader, who was regarded as the messenger of God. For such men there were no different degrees of sinfulness—some were held to be elect or " chosen of the Lord " at their birth, while others were predestined for everlasting punishment It was characteristic of Calvin that he called vehemently for toleration from the Emperor, Charles V, and yet caused the death of a Spanish physician, Servetus, whose views happened to be at variance with his own !

The Calvinists generally held meetings in the open air where they could escape the restrictions that were placed on services held in any place of worship. The middle and lower classes attended them in large numbers, and the new faith spread rapidly through the enlightened world of Western Europe. John Knox, the renowned Scotch preacher, was a firm friend of Calvin, and thundered denunciations from his Scotch pulpit at the young Queen Mary, who had come from France with all the levity of French court-training in her manners. The people of Southern France were eager to hear the fiery speech that somehow captured their imagination. As they increased in numbers and began to have political importance they became known as Huguenots or Confederates. To Catherine de Medici, the Catholic Regent of France, they were a formidable body, and in Navarre their leaders were drawn mainly from the nobles.

Relentless persecution would probably have crushed the Huguenots of France eventually if it had been equally severe in all cases. As a rule, men of the highest rank could evade punishment, and a few of the higher clergy preached religious toleration. Thousands marched cheerfully to death from among the ranks of humble citizens, for it was part of Calvin's creed that men ought to suffer martyrdom for their faith without offering resistance. Judges were known to die, stricken by remorse, and marvelling at their victims' fortitude. At Dijon, the executioner himself proclaimed at the foot of the scaffold that he had been converted.

The Calvinist preachers could gain no audience in Paris, where the University of the Sorbonne opposed their doctrines and declared that these were contrary to all the philosophy of ancient times. The capital of France constantly proclaimed loyalty to Rome by the pompous processions which filed out of its magnificent churches and paraded the streets to awe the mob, always swayed by the violence of fanatic priests. The Huguenots did not attempt to capture a stronghold, where it was boasted that "the novices of the convents and the priests' housekeepers could have driven them out with broomsticks."

Such rude weapons would have been ineffectual in the South-East of France, where all the most flourishing towns had embraced the reformed religion. The majority of the Huguenots were drawn from the most warlike, intelligent, and industrious of the population of these towns, but princes also adopted Calvinism, and the Bourbons of Navarre made their court a refuge for believers in the new religion.

Navarre was at this time a narrow strip of land on the French side of the Pyrenees, but her ruler was still a sovereign monarch and owed allegiance to no overlord. Henry, Prince of Bourbon and King of Navarre, was born in 1555 at Béarns, in the mountains. His mother was a Calvinist, and his early discipline was rigid. He ran barefoot with the village lads, learnt to climb like a chamois, and knew nothing more luxurious than the habits of a court which had become enamoured of simplicity. He was bewildered on his introduction to the shameless, intriguing circle of Catherine de Medici.

The Queen-Mother did not allow King Charles IX to have much share in the government of France at that period. She had an Italian love of dissimulation, and followed the methods of the rulers of petty Italian states in her policy, which was to play off one rival faction against another. Henry of Guise led the Catholic party against the Huguenots, whose leaders were Prince Louis de Bourbon and his uncle, the noble Admiral de Coligny. Guise was so determined to gain power that he actually asked the help of Spain in his attempt to crush the " heretics " of his own nation.

The Huguenots at that time had won many notable concessions from the Crown, which increased the bitter hostility of the Catholics. The Queen-Mother, however, concealed her annoyance when she saw the ladies of the court reading the New Testament instead of pagan poetry, or heard their voices chanting godly psalms rather than the old love-ballads. She did not object openly to the pious form of speech which was known as the "language of Canaan." She was a passionless woman, self-seeking but not revengeful, and adopted a certain degree of tolerance, no doubt, from her patriotic counsellor, L'Hôpital, who resembled the Prince of Orange in his character.

The Edict of January in 1562 gave countenance to Huguenot meetings throughout France, and was, therefore, detested by the Catholic party. The Duke of Guise went to dine one Sunday in the little town of Vassy, near his residence of Joinville. A band of armed retainers accompanied him and pushed their way into a barn where the Huguenots were holding service. A riot ensued, in which the Duke was struck, and his followers killed no less than sixty of the worshippers.

This outrage led to civil war, for the Protestants remembered bitterly that Guise had sworn never to take life in the cause of religion. They demanded the punishment of the offenders, and then took the field most valiantly. Gentlemen served at their own expense, but they were, in general, "better armed with courage than with corselets." They were overpowered by the numbers of the Catholic League, which had all the wealth of Church and State at its back, and also had control of the King and capital. One by one the heroic leaders fell. Louis de Bourbon was taken prisoner at Dreux, and Anthony of Bourbon died before the town of Rouen.

The Queen of Navarre was very anxious for the safety of her son, for she heard that he was accompanying

Catherine and Charles IX on a long progress through the kingdom. She herself was the object of Catholic animosity, and the King of Spain destined her for a grand *Auto-da-fé*, longing to make an example of so proud a heretic. She believed that her son had received the root of piety in his heart while he was under her care, but she doubted whether that goodly root would grow in the corrupt atmosphere which surrounded the youthful Valois princes. Henry of Navarre disliked learning, and was fond of active exercise. His education was varied after he came to court, and he learnt to read men well. In later life he was able to enjoy the most frivolous pastimes and yet could endure the privations of camp life without experiencing discomfort.

Louis de Bourbon, Prince de Condé, was killed at the battle of Jarnac, and Henry de Bourbon became the recognized head of the Huguenot party. He took an oath never to abandon the cause, and was hailed by the soldiers in camp as their future leader. The Queen of Navarre clad him in his armour, delighted that her son should defend the reformed religion. She saw that he was brave and manly, if he were not a truly religious prince, and she agreed with the loudly expressed opinion of the populace that he was more royal in bearing than the dissolute and effeminate youths who spent their idle days within the palaces of the Louvre and the Tuileries.

The country was growing so weary of the struggle that the scheme for a marriage between Henry of Navarre and Margaret of Valois was hailed with enthusiasm. If Catholic and Huguenot were united there might be peace in France that would add to the prosperity of the nation. Catherine de Medici had intended originally that her daughter should marry the

Catholic King of Portugal, and was angry with Philip II of Spain because he had done nothing to assist her in making this alliance. Charles IX longed to humble Philip, who was indignant that the "heretics" had been offered freedom of worship in 1570, and had expressed his opinion rather freely. Therefore the Valois family did not hesitate to receive the leader of the Protestants, Henry de Bourbon, whose territory extended from the Pyrenees to far beyond the Garonne.

The Queen of Navarre disliked the match and was suspicious of the Queen-Mother's motives. She feared that Catherine and Catherine's daughter would entice Henry into a gay, dissolute course of life which would destroy the results of her early training, and she could not respond very cordially to the effusive welcome which greeted her at the court when she came sadly to the wedding.

The marriage contract was signed in 1571, neither bride nor bridegroom having much choice in the matter. Henry was probably dazzled by the brilliant prospects that opened out to one who was mated with a Valois, but he was only nineteen and never quite at ease in the shifting, tortuous maze of diplomacy as conceived by the mind of Catherine de Medici. Margaret was a talented, lively girl, and pleased with the fine jewels that were given her. She did not understand the reasons which urged her brother Charles to press on the match. He insisted that it should take place in Paris in order that he might show his subjects how much he longed to settle the religious strife that had lately rent the kingdom. It was a question, of course, on which neither of the contracting parties had to be more than formally consulted.

The Queen of Navarre died suddenly on the eve of

the wedding, and her son, with 800 attendants, entered the city in a mourning garb that had soon to be discarded. Gorgeous costumes of ceremony were donned for the great day, August 18th, 1572, when Margaret met her bridegroom on a great stage erected before the church of Notre Dame.

Henry of Navarre could not attend the Mass, but walked in the nave with his Huguenot friends, while Margaret knelt in the choir, surrounded by the Catholics of the party. Admiral Coligny was present, the stalwart Huguenot who appealed to all the finest instincts of his people. He had tried to arrange a marriage between Elizabeth of England and Henry of Anjou, the brother of the French King, but had not been successful, owing to Elizabeth's politic vacillation. He was detested by Catherine de Medici because he had great power over her son, the reigning monarch, whom she tried to dominate completely. A dark design had inspired the Guise faction of late in consequence of the Queen's enmity to the influence of Coligny. It was hinted that the Huguenot party would be very weak if their strongest partisan were suddenly taken from them. All the great Protestant nobles were assembled in Paris for the marriage of Navarre and Margaret of Valois. They were royally entertained by the Catholic courtiers and lodged at night in fine apartments of the Louvre and other palaces. They had no idea that they had any danger to fear as they slept, and would have disdained to guard themselves against the possible treachery of their hosts. They might have been warned by the attempted assassination of Admiral Coligny, who was wounded by a pistol-shot, had not the King expressed such concern at the attempt on the life of his favourite counsellor. "My father," Charles IX declared when he came to the Admiral's bedside, " the pain of the wound is yours, but the insult and the wrong are mine."

The King had the gates of Paris shut, and sent his own guard to protect Coligny. He was weak, and subject to violent gusts of passion which made him easy to guide, if he were in the hands of an unscrupulous person. His mother, who had plotted with Guise for the death of Coligny, pointed out that there was grave danger to be feared from the Protestants. She made Charles declare in a frenzy of violence that every Huguenot in France should perish if the Admiral died, for he would not be reproached with such a crime by the Admiral's followers.

The bells of the church nearest to the Louvre rang out on the Eve of St Bartholomew—they gave the signal for a cruel massacre. After the devout Protestant, Coligny, was slain in the presence of the Duke of Guise, there was little resistance from the other defenceless Huguenot nobles. They were roused from sleep, surprised by treacherous foes, and relentlessly murdered. It was impossible to combine in their perilous position. Two thousand were put to death in Paris, where the very women and children acted like monsters of cruelty to the heretics for three days, and proved themselves as cunning as the Swiss guards who had slain the King's guests on the night of Saint Bartholomew. A Huguenot noble escaped from his assailants and rushed into Henry's very bridal chamber. He cried, " Navarre ! Navarre ! " and hoped for protection from the Protestant prince against four archers who were following him. Henry had risen early and gone out to the tennis-court, and Margaret was powerless to offer any help. She fled from the room in terror, having heard nothing previously of the Guises' secret conspiracy.

Charles IX sent for Navarre and disclosed the fact that he had been privy to the massacre. He showed plainly that the Protestants were to find no toleration henceforth. Henry felt that his life was in great jeopardy, for most of the noblemen he had brought to Paris had fallen in the massacre, and he stood practically alone at a Catholic court. Henry understood that if he were to be spared it was only at the price of his conversion, and with the alternatives of death or the Mass before him, it is little wonder that he yielded, at least in appearance, to the latter. There were spies and traitors to be feared in the circle of the Medici. Even Margaret was not safe since her marriage to a Protestant, but she gave wise counsel to her husband and guided him skilfully through the perils of court life.

Catherine disarmed the general indignation of Europe by spreading an ingeniously concocted story to the effect that the Huguenots had been sacrificed because they plotted a foul attack on the Crown of France. She had been hostile to Coligny rather than to his policy, and continued to follow his scheme of thwarting Spain by alliances with Elizabeth and the Prince of Orange.

Henry of Guise met the charge of excessive zeal in defending his King with perfect equanimity. He was a splendid figure at the court, winning popularity by his affable manners and managing to conceal his arrogant, ambitious nature.

After 1572 the Huguenots relied mainly on the wealthy citizens of the towns for support in the struggle against the Guise faction. In addition to religious toleration they now demanded the redress of political grievances. A republican spirit rose in the Protestant party, who read eagerly the various books and pamphlets declaring that a monarchy should not continue if it proved incapable of maintaining order even by despotic powers. More and more a new idea gained ground that the sovereignty of France was not hereditary but elective.

Charles IX, distracted by the confusion in his kingdom and the caprices of his own ill-balanced temper, clung to Henry of Navarre because he recognized real strength in him such as was wanting in the Valois. Henry III, his successor, was contemptibly vain and feminine in all his tastes, wearing pearls in his hair and rouging his face in order that he might be admired by the foolish, empty courtiers who were his favourite companions. He succeeded to the throne in 1575, and made some display of Catholic zeal by organizing fantastic processions of repentant sinners through the streets of Paris. He insisted on Navarre taking part in this mummery, for it was to his interest to prevent the Protestant party from claiming a noble leader.

Navarre had learnt to play his part well, but he chafed at his inglorious position. He saw with a fierce disgust the worthless prince, Alençon, become the head of the Protestant party. Then he discovered that he was to have a chance of escape from the toils of the Medici. In January, 1576, he received an offer from some officers—who had been disappointed of the royal favour—that they would put him in possession of certain towns if he would leave the court. He rode off at once to the Protestant camp, leaving his wife behind him.

The Peace of Monsieur, signed in February 1576, granted very favourable conditions to the Protestants, who had stoutly resisted an attack on their stronghold of La Rochelle. Catherine and Henry III became alarmed by the increasing numbers of their enemies, for a Catholic League was formed by Henry of Guise and other discontented subjects in order to ally Paris with the fanatics of the provinces. This League was by no means favourable to the King and Catherine, for its openly avowed leader was Henry of Guise, who was greatly beloved by the people. Henry III was foolish enough to become a member, thereby incurring some loss of prestige by placing himself practically under the authority of his rival. Bitterly hostile to the Protestants as were the aims of the League, it was nevertheless largely used by the Duke of Guise as a cloak to cover his designs for the usurpation of the royal power. The hope of Henry III and his mother was that the rival Catholics and Protestants would fight out their own quarrel and leave the Crown to watch the battles unmolested.

The last of the Valois was closely watched by the bold preachers of political emancipation. These were determined to snatch the royal prerogatives from him if he were unworthy of respect and squandered too much public money on his follies. It enraged them to hear that he spent hours on his own toilette, and starched his wife's fine ruffs as if he were her tire-woman. They were angry when they were told that their King regarded his functions so lightly that he gave audiences to ambassadors with a basketful of puppies round his neck, and did not trouble to read the reports his ministers sent to him. They decided secretly to proclaim Henry III's kinsman, the King of Navarre, who was a fine soldier and a kindly, humane gentleman.

Navarre was openly welcomed as the leader of the Reformed Church party. He was readmitted to Calvinist communion, and abjured the Mass. He took the field gladly, being delighted to remove the mask he had been obliged to wear. His brilliant feats of arms made him more popular than ever.

When Anjou died, Navarre was heir presumptive to the throne, and had to meet the furious hostility of the Guise faction. These said that Navarre's uncle, Cardinal de Bourbon, " a wine-tun rather than a man," should be their king when Valois died. They secured the help of Spain before publishing their famous Manifesto. This document avowed the intentions of those forming the Catholic League to restore the dignity of the Church by drawing the sword, if necessary, and to settle for themselves the question of Henry III's successor. He bribed the people by releasing them from taxation and promised regular meetings of the States-General.

The King hesitated to grant the League's demands, which were definitely formulated in 1585. He did not wish to revoke the Edicts of Toleration that had recently been passed, and might have refused, if his mother had not advised him to make every concession that was possible to avoid the enmity of the Guise faction. He consented, and was lost, for the Huguenots sprang to arms, and he found that he was to be driven from his capital by the Guises.

The King was accused of sympathy with the Protestant cause, which made his name odious to the Catholic University of Paris. He had personal enemies too, such as the Duchess of Montpensier, sister to Henry of Guise, who was fond of saying that she would give him another crown by using the gold scissors at her waist. There was some talk of his entering a monastery where he would have had to adopt the tonsure.

One-half of Navarre's beard had turned white when he heard that Henry III was revoking the Edicts of Toleration. Yet he was happiest in camp, and leapt to the saddle with a light heart in May 1588 when the

King fled from Paris and Guise entered the capital as the deliverer of the people. He looked the model of a Gascon knight, with hooked nose and bold, black eyes under ironical arched eyebrows. He was a clever judge of character, and knew how to win adherents to his cause His homely garb attracted many who were tired of the weak Valois kings, for there was no artificial grace in the scarlet cloak, brown velvet doublet and white-plumed hat which distinguished him from his fellows.

Henry III plotted desperately to regain his prestige, and showed some of the Medici guile in a plot for Guise's assassination. When this succeeded he went to boast to Catherine that he had killed the King of Paris. " You have cut boldly into the stuff, my son," she answered him, " but will you know how to sew it together ? "

Paris was filled by lamentations for the death of Guise, and the festivities of Christmas Eve gave way to funeral dirges. The University of Sorbonne declared that they would not receive Henry of Valois again as king. His only hope was to reconcile himself with Navarre and the Protestant party. Paris was tumultuous with resistance when the news came that Royalists and Huguenots had raised their standards in the same camp and massed two armies. The Catholic League was beloved by the poorer citizens because it released them from rent-dues. The spirit of the people was shown by processions of children, who threw lighted torches to the ground before the churches, stamped on them, and cried, " Thus may God quench the House of Valois ! "

The capital welcomed Spanish troops to aid them in keeping Henry III from the gates. He was assassinated by a Burgundian monk as he approached the city " he had loved more than his wife," and Henry of Navarre, though a heretic, now claimed the right of entrance.

Navarre was the lineal descendant of Saint Louis of France, but for ten generations no ancestor of his in the male line had ruled the French kingdom. He was the grandson of Margaret, sister of Francis I, and Henry d'Albret, who had borne captivity with that monarch. Many were pledged to him by vows made to the dying King, who had come to look on him as a doughty champion; many swore that they would die a thousand deaths rather than be the servants of a heretic master.

In February 1590, Henry laid siege to Dreux in order to place himself between his enemies and Paris. Mayenne, the leader of the opposite camp, drew him to Ivry, where a battle was fought on March 14th, resulting in the complete discomfiture of the Catholic Leaguers. The white plume of Navarre floated victorious on the field, and the black lilies of Mayenne were trampled. The road to Paris lay open to the heretic King, who invested the city on the northern side, but did not attack the inhabitants. The blockade would have reduced the hungry citizens to submission at the end of a month if the Duke of Parma had not come to their relief at the command of the Spanish sovereign.

Philip II wished his daughter to marry the young Duke of Guise and to ascend the French throne with her husband. For that reason he supported Paris in its refusal to accept the Protestant King of Navarre. It was not till March 1594, that the King, known as Henri Quatre, was able to lead his troops into Paris.

Navarre had been compelled to attend Mass in public and to ask absolution from the Archbishop of Bourges, who received him into the fold of the Catholic, Apostolic and Roman Church before the coronation. He was now the " most Christian King," welcomed with blaze of bonfires and the blare of trumpets. He was crowned at Chartres because the Catholic League held Rheims, and he entered Paris by the Porte Neuve, through which Henry III had fled from the Guises some six years previously. The Spaniards had to withdraw from his capital, being told that their services would be required no longer.

Henry IV waged successful wars against Spain and the Catholic League, gradually recovering the whole of his dominions by his energy and courage. He settled the status of the Protestants on a satisfactory basis by the Edict of Nantes, which was signed in April 1598, to consolidate the privileges which had been previously granted to the Calvinists. Full civil rights and full civil protection were granted to all Protestants, and the King assigned a sum of money for the use of Protestant schools and colleges.

Henry introduced the silk industry into France, and his famous minister, Sully, did much to improve the condition of French agriculture. By 1598 order had been restored in the kingdom, but industry and commerce had been crippled by nearly forty years of civil war. When France's first Bourbon King, Henry IV, was assassinated in April 1610, he had only begun the great work of social and economical reform which proved his genuine sense of public duty.

Chapter X

Under the Red Robe

NEVER was king more beloved by his subjects than Henry of Navarre, who had so many of the frank and genial qualities which his nation valued. There was mourning as for a father when the fanatic, Ravaillac, struck him to the ground. It seemed strange that death should come in the same guise to the first of the Bourbon line and the last of the Valois.

Henry had studied the welfare of the peasantry and the middle class, striving to crush the power of the nobles whose hands were perpetually raised one against the other. Therefore he intrusted affairs of State to men of inferior rank, and determined that he would form in France a nobility of the robe that should equal the old nobility of the sword. The *paulette* gave to all those who held the higher judicial functions of the State the right to transmit their offices by will to their descendants, or even to sell them as so much hereditary property.

In foreign affairs Henry had attempted to check the ambitious schemes of the Spanish Hapsburg line and to restore the ancient prestige of France in Europe, but he had to leave his country in a critical stage and hope that a man would be found to carry on his great work. Cardinal Richelieu was to have the supreme honour of fulfilling Henry IV's designs, with the energy of a nature that had otherwise very little in common with that of the first King of the Bourbons.

Armand Jean Duplessis, born in 1585, was the youngest son of François Duplessis, knight of Richelieu, who fought for Navarre upon the battle-fields of Arques and Ivry. He was naturally destined for a military career, and had seen, when he was a little child, some of the terrible scenes of the religious wars. Peering from the window of the château in the sad, desolate land of Poitou, he caught glimpses of ragged regiments of French troops, or saw foreign soldiers in their unfamiliar garb, intent on pillaging the mean huts of the peasantry. Armand was sent to Paris at an early age that he might study at the famous College of Navarre, where the youths of the day were well equipped for court life. He learned Spanish in addition to Latin and Greek, and became an adept in riding, dancing and fencing. When he left the humble student quarter of the capital and began to mingle with the crowd who formed the court, he soon put off the manners of a rustic and acquired the polished elegance of a courtier of the period. He spent much time in studying the drama of Parisian daily life, a brilliant, shifting series of gay scenes, with the revelation now and then of a cruel and sordid background.

The very sounds of active life must at first have startled the dreamy youth who had come from the seclusion of a château in the marsh land. Cavaliers in velvet and satin rallied to the roll of a drum which the soldiers beat in martial-wise, and engaged in fierce conflicts with each other. Acts were constantly passed to forbid duelling, but there were many wounded every year in the streets, and the nobility would have thought themselves disgraced if they had not drawn their swords readily in answer to an insult. Class distinctions were observed rigidly, and the merchant clad in hodden grey and the lawyer robed in black were pushed aside with some contempt when there was any conflict between the aristocrats. The busy Pont Neuf seemed to be the bridge which joined two different worlds. Here monks rubbed shoulders with yellow-garbed Jews, and ladies of the court tripped side by side with the gay *filles* of the town. Anyone strolling near the river Seine could watch, if he chose, the multicoloured throng and amuse himself by the contrast between the different phases of society in Paris.

Richelieu, who held the proud title of Marquis de Chillon, handled a sword skilfully and dreamed of glory won upon battle-fields. He was dismayed when he first heard that his widowed mother had changed her plans for his career. A brother, who was to have been consecrated Bishop of Luçon, had decided to turn monk, and as the preferment to the See was in the hands of the family, it had been decided that Armand Jean should have the benefit.

Soon a fresh vision had formed before the eyes of the handsome Bishop, who visited Rome and made friends among the highest dignitaries. He was tall and slender, with an oval face and the keenest of grey eyes; rich black hair fell to his shoulders and a pointed beard lent distinction to his face. The Louvre and the Vatican approved him, and many protesting voices were heard when Richelieu went down to his country diocese.

Poitou was one of the poorest districts of France, the peasants being glad enough to get bread and chestnuts for their main food. The cathedral was battered by warfare and the palace very wretched. Orders to

Parisian merchants made the last habitable, Richelieu declaring that, although a beggar, he had need of silver plates and such luxuries to "enhance his nobility." The first work he had found to do was done very thoroughly. He set the place in order and conciliated the Huguenots. Then he demanded relief from taxation for his overburdened flock, writing urgently to headquarters on this subject. He had much vexation to overcome whenever he came into contact with the priests drawn from the peasantry. These were far too fond of gambling and drinking in the ale-houses, and had to be prohibited from celebrating marriages by night, a custom that led to many scandals.

But Luçon was soon too narrow a sphere for the energy and ambition of a Richelieu. The Bishop longed to establish himself in a palace "near to that of God and that of the King," for he combined worldly wisdom with a zeal for religious purity. He happened to welcome the royal procession that was setting out for Spain on the occasion of Louis XIII's marriage to Anne of Austria, a daughter of Philip II. He made so noble an impression of hospitality that he was rewarded by the post of Almoner to the new Queen and was placed upon the Regent's Council.

Richelieu had watched the coronation of the quiet boy of fourteen in the cathedral of Notre Dame, for he had walked in the state procession. He knew that Louis XIII was a mere cipher, fond of hunting and loth to appear in public. Marie de Medici, the Regent, was the prime mover of intrigues. It was wise to gain her favour and the friendship of her real rulers, the Italian Concini.

Concini himself was noble by birth, whereas his wife, the sallow, deformed Leonora, was the daughter of a laundress who had nursed the Queen in illness. Both were extravagant, costing the Crown enormous sums of money—Leonora had a pretty taste in jewels as well as clothes, and Marie de Medici even plundered the Bastille of her husband's hoards because she could deny her favourites nothing.

Richelieu rose to eminence in the gay, luxurious court where the weak, vain Florentine presided. He had ousted other men, and feared for his own safety when the Concini were attacked by their exasperated opponents. Concini himself was shot, and his wife was lodged in the Bastille on a charge of sorcery. Paris rejoiced in the fall of these Italian parasites, and Marie de Medici shed no tears for them. She turned to her secretary, Richelieu, when she was driven from the court and implored him to mediate for her with Louis XIII and his favourite sportsman-adventurer, de Luynes, who had originally been employed to teach the young King falconry.

Richelieu went to the château of Blois where Marie de Medici had fled, a royal exile, but he received orders from Luynes, who was in power, to proceed to Luçon and guide his flock " to observe the commandments of God and the King." The Bishop was exceedingly provoked by the taunt, but he was obliged to wait for better fortunes. Marie was plotting after the manner of the Florentines, but her plans were generally fruitless. She managed to escape from Blois with Epérnon, the general of Henry IV, and despite a solemn oath that she would live " in entire resignation to the King's will," she would have had civil war against the King and his adviser.

Richelieu managed to make peace and brought about the marriage of his beautiful young kinswoman to the Marquis of Cambalet, who was de Luynes' nephew. He did not, however, receive the Cardinal's Hat, which had become the chief object of his personal ambition.

The minister, de Luynes, became so unpopular, at length, that his enemies found it possible to retaliate. He favoured the Spanish alliance, whereas many wished to help the Protestants of Germany in their struggle to uphold Frederick, the Elector Palatine, against Ferdinand of Bohemia. The Huguenots rose in the south, and Luynes took the field desperately, for he knew that anything but victory would be fatal to his own fortunes. Songs were shouted in the Paris taverns, satirizing his weak government. Richelieu had bought the service of a host of scribblers in the mean streets near the Place Royale, and these were virulent in verse and pamphlet, according to the dictates of their master.

Fever carried off de Luynes, and the valets who played cards on his coffin were hardly more indecent in their callousness than de Luynes' enemies. The Cardinal's Hat arrived with many gracious compliments to the Bishop of Luçon, who then gave up his diocese. Soon he rustled in flame-coloured taffeta at fêtes and receptions, for wealth and all the rewards of office came to him. As a Prince of the Church, he claimed precedence of princes of the blood, and was hardly astonished when the King requested him to form a ministry. In that ministry the power of the Cardinal was supreme, and he had friends in all posts of importance. With a show of reluctance he entered on his life-work. It was a great and patriotic task—no less than the aggrandisement of France in Europe.

France must be united if she were to present a solid front against the Spanish vengeance that would threaten any change of policy. The Queen-Regent had intended to support Rome, Austria and Spain against the Protestant forces of the northern countries. Richelieu determined to change that plan, but he knew that the time was not yet ripe, since he had neither a fleet nor an army to defeat such adversaries.

The Huguenot faction must be ruined in order that France might not be torn by internal struggles. The new French army was sent to surround La Rochelle, the Protestant fort, which expected help from England. The English fleet tried for fourteen days to relieve the garrison, but had to sail away defeated. The sailors of the town elected one of their number to be Mayor, a rough pirate who was unwilling to assume the office. "I don't want to be Mayor," he cried, flinging his knife upon the Council-Table, "but, since you want it, there is my knife for the first man who talks of surrender." The spirit of resistance within the walls of La Rochelle rose after this declaration. The citizens continued to defy the besiegers until a bushel of corn cost 1,000 livres and an ordinary household cat could be sold for forty-five!

It was Richelieu's intention to starve the inhabitants of La Rochelle into surrender. He had his will, being a man of iron, and held Mass in the Protestant stronghold. He treated the people well, allowing them freedom of religion, but he razed both the fort and the walls to the ground and took away all their political privileges. The Huguenots were too grateful for the liberty that was left to them to menace the French Government any longer. Most of them were loyal citizens and helped the Cardinal to maintain peace. In any case they did not exist as a separate political party.

Richelieu reduced the power of the nobles by relentless

measures that struck at their feudal independence. No fortresses were to be held by them unless they lived on the frontiers of France, where some defence was necessary against a foreign enemy. When their strong castles were pulled down, the great lords seemed to have lost much of their ancient dignity. They were forbidden to duel, and dared not disobey the law after they had seen the guilty brought relentlessly to the scaffold. The first families of France had to acknowledge a superior in the mighty Cardinal Richelieu. Intendants were sent out to govern provinces and diminish the local influence of the landlords. Most of these were men of inferior rank to the nobility, who found themselves compelled to go to the wars if they wished to earn distinction. The result was good, for it added many recruits to the land and sea forces.

In 1629, the Cardinal donned sword and cuirass and led out the royal army to the support of the Duke of Mantua, a French nobleman who had inherited an Italian duchy and found his rights disputed by both Spain and Savoy. Louis XIII accompanied Richelieu and showed himself a brave soldier. Their road to Italy was by the Pass of Susa, thick with snow in the early spring and dangerous from the presence of Savoy's hostile troups. They forced their way into Italy, and there Richelieu remained to make terms with the enemy, while Louis returned to his kingdom.

Richelieu induced both Spain and Savoy to acknowledge the rights of the Duke of Mantua, and then turned his attention to the resistance which had been organized in Southern France by the Protestants under the Duke of Rohan. The latter had obtained promises of aid from Charles I of England and Philip IV of Spain, but found that his allies deserted him at a critical moment and left him to face the formidable army of the Cardinal. The Huguenots submitted to their fate in the summer of 1629, finding themselves in a worse plight than they had been when they surrendered La Rochelle, for Richelieu treated with them no longer as with a foreign power. He expected them to offer him the servile obedience of conquered rebels. Henceforth he exerted himself to restore the full supremacy of the Catholic faith in France by making as many converts as was possible and by opening Jesuit and Capuchin missions in the Protestant places. " Some were brought to see the truth by fear and some by favour." Yet Richelieu did not play the part of a persecutor in the State, for he was afraid of weakening France by driving away heretics who might help to increase her strength in foreign warfare. He was pleased to find so many of the Huguenots loyal to their King, and rejoiced that there would never be the possibility of some discontented nobleman rising against his rule with a Protestant force in the background. The Huguenots devoted their time to peaceful worship after their own mind, and waxed very prosperous through their steady pursuit of commerce

Richelieu returned to France in triumph, having won amazing success in his three years' struggle. He had personal enemies on every side, but for the moment these were silenced. " In the eyes of the world, he was the foremost man in France." For nineteen years he was to be the King's chief minister, although he was many times in peril of losing credit, and even life itself, through the jealous envy of his superiors and fellow-subjects.

Mary de Medici forsook the man she had raised to some degree of eminence, and declared that he had shown himself ungrateful. The nobility in general felt his power tyrannical, and the clergy thought that he sacrificed the Church to the interests of the State in politics. Louis XIII was restive sometimes under the heavy hand of the Cardinal, who dared to point out the royal weaknesses and to insist that he should try to overcome them.

Richelieu was very skilful in avoiding the pitfalls that beset his path as statesman. He had many spies in his service, paid to bring him reports of his enemies' speech and actions. Great ladies of the court did not disdain to betray their friends, and priests even advised penitents in the Confessional to act as the Cardinal wished them. When any treachery was discovered, it was punished swiftly. The Cardinal refused to spare men of the highest rank who plotted against the King or his ministers, for he had seen the dangers of revolt and decided to stamp it out relentlessly. Some strain of chivalry forbade him to treat women with the same severity he showed to male conspirators. He had a cunning adversary in one Madame de Chevreuse, who would ride with the fearless speed of a man to outwit any scheme of Richelieu.

The life of a king in feeble health was all that stood between the Cardinal and ruin, and several times it seemed impossible that he should outwit his enemies. Louis XIII fell ill in 1630. At the end of September he was not expected to survive, and the physicians bade him attend to his soul's welfare.

The Cardinal's enemies exulted, openly declaring that the King's adviser should die with the King. The heir to the throne was Louis' brother Gaston, a weak and cowardly prince, who detested the minister in office and hoped to overthrow him. When the sufferer

An Application to the Cardinal for his Favour
Walter Gay

recovered there was much disappointment to be concealed. The Queen-Mother had set her heart on Marillac being made head of the army in Richelieu's place, and had secret designs to make Marillac's brother, then the guard of the seals, the chief minister.

Louis was induced to say that he would dismiss the Cardinal when he was completely recovered from his illness, but he did not feel himself bound by the promise when he had rid himself of Marie de Medici and felt once again the influence of Richelieu. He went to Versailles to hunt on November 11th, 1630, and there met the Cardinal, who was able to convince him that it would be best for the interests of France to have a strong and dauntless minister dominating all the petty offices in the State instead of a number of incapable, greedy intriguers such as would be appointed by Marie de Medici. On this Day of Dupes the court was over-confident of success, believing that the Cardinal had fled from the disgrace that would shortly overtake him. The joy of the courtiers was banished by a message that Marillac was to be dismissed. The Queen-Mother knew at once that her schemes had failed, and that her son had extricated himself from her toils that he might retain Richelieu.

Marshal Marillac and his brother were both condemned to death. Another noble, Bassompierre, was arrested and put in the Bastille because he was known to have sympathized with the Cardinal's enemies. Richelieu did not rid himself so easily of Marie de Medici, who was his deadliest enemy. She went into banishment voluntarily, but continued to devise many plots with the Spanish enemies of France, for she had no scruples in availing herself of foreign help against the hated minister.

After the Day of Dupes, Richelieu grasped the reins of government more firmly. He asked no advice, and feared no opposition to his rule. His foreign policy differed from that pursued by Marie de Medici, because he realized that France could never lead the continental powers until she had checked the arrogance of Spanish claims to supremacy. It seems strange that he should support the Protestant princes of Germany against their Catholic Emperor when the Thirty Years' War broke out, but it must be remembered that the Emperor, Ferdinand II, was closely allied to the King of Spain, and that the success of the former would mean a second powerful Catholic State in Europe. The House of Austria was already strong and menaced France in her struggle for ascendancy.

In 1635, war was formally declared by France against the Emperor Ferdinand and Spain. Richelieu did not live to see the conclusion of this war, but he had the satisfaction of knowing that, at its close, France would be established as the foremost of European nations, and he felt that the result would be worth a lavish expenditure of men and money. In 1636, France was threatened by a Spanish invasion, which alarmed the people of the capital so terribly that they attacked the minister who had plunged them into warfare. Richelieu displayed great courage and inspired a patriotic rising, the syndics of the various trades waiting on the King to offer lavish contributions in aid of the defence of Paris. Louis took the field at the head of a fine army which was largely composed of eager volunteers, and the national danger was averted.

Harassed by the cares of war, the Cardinal delighted in the gratitude of men of letters whom he took under his protection. He founded the famous Academy of

France and had his own plays performed at Ruel, the century-old château, where he gave fêtes of great magnificence. His niece, Mme. de Cambalet, was made Duchesse D'Aiguillon that she might adorn the sphere in which the Cardinal moved so royally. She was a beautiful woman of simple tastes, and yearned for a life of conventual seclusion as she received the homage of Corneille or visited the salon of the brilliant wit, Julie de Rambouillet.

Richelieu had a dozen estates in different parts of France and spent vast sums on their splendid maintenance. He adorned the home of his ancestors with art treasures—pictures by Poussin, bronzes from Greece and Italy, and the statuary of Michael Angelo. His own equestrian statue was placed side by side with that of Louis XIII because they had ridden together to great victory. The King survived his minister only a few months; Richelieu died on December 4th, 1642, and Louis XIII in the following May. They left the people of France submissive to an absolute monarchy.

Chapter XI

The Grand Monarch

RICHELIEU bequeathed his famous Palais Cardinal to the royal family of France. He left the reins of tyranny in the hands of Mazarin, a Spaniard, who had complete ascendancy over the so-called Regent, Anne of Austria.

There was not much state in the magnificent palace of little Louis XIV during his long minority, and he chafed against the restrictions of a parsimonious household. Mazarin was bent on amassing riches for himself and would not untie the purse-strings even for those gala-days on which the court was expected to be gorgeous. He stinted the education of the heir to the Crown, fearing that a well-equipped youth would demand the right to govern for himself. His system was so successful in the end that the mightiest of the Bourbon kings could barely read and write.

Yet Louis XIV grew strong and handsome, with a superb bearing that was not concealed by his shabby clothes, and a dauntless arrogance that resented all slights on the royal prerogative. He refused to drive in the dilapidated equipage which had been provided for his use, and made such a firm stand against Mazarin's avarice in this case that five new carriages were ordered.

The populace rose, too, against the first minister of the State, whose wealth had increased enormously

The Grand Monarch

through his exactions from the poorer classes. France was full of abuses that Richelieu himself had scarcely tried to sweep away. The peasants laboured under heavy burdens, the roads were dangerous for all travellers, and the streets of cities were infested after nightfall by dangerous pickpockets and assassins. There had been a great victory won at Rocroy by the Duc d'Enghien, who routed the Spanish and sent two hundred and sixty standards to the church of Notre Dame; but this glorious feat of arms brought neither food nor clothing to the poor, and the fierce internal strife, known as La Fronde, broke out. The very name was undignified, being derived from a kind of sling used by the urchins of the Paris streets. It was a mere series of brawls between Frondeurs and Mazarins, and brought much humiliation to the State.

In 1649, civil war began which withdrew France somewhat from European broils. Enghien (Condé) returned to Paris to range himself against the unruly Parlement as leader of the court party, and to try to reduce Paris by a military force. When the capital was besieged Anne of Austria had to retire to Saint-Germains with her son, who suffered the indignity of sleeping on a bed of straw in those troubled times. She concluded peace rather thankfully in March when the besieged citizens had suffered severely from want of food. The young King showed himself in Paris in August when the tumult was at its worst, for the troubles of King Charles I of England incited the Frondeurs to persevere in their desire for a French Republic, where no minister should exercise the royal prerogatives.

Mazarin played a losing game, and went into exile when Louis XIV was declared of age. The young King was only thirteen but had the dignity of manhood in his air and carriage, and showed no fear in accepting absolute power. But it was not until ten years later that he was finally freed from Mazarin. When the cardinal was dead he proclaimed his future policy to the state of France—" Gentlemen," said he, " I shall be my own prime minister."

In November 1659, the Treaty of the Pyrenees had restored peace to France and Spain. In the following year Louis XIV wedded the Infanta, daughter of Philip IV, who renounced all her prospective rights to the Spanish crown. Mazarin had done well for France in these last diplomatic efforts for the crown, but he had forced the people to contribute to the enormous fortune which he made over to the King.

Colbert was the indefatigable minister who aided the new monarch to restore the dignity of court life in France. He revealed vast hoards which the crafty Mazarin had concealed, and formed schemes of splendour that should be worthy of a splendid king.

Louis XIV was one of the richest monarchs of Christendom, with a taste for royal pomp that could be gratified only by an enormous display of wealth. He wished the distasteful scenes of his early life to be forgotten by his subjects, and decided to build himself a residence that would form a fitting background for his own magnificence. He would no longer live within the walls of Paris, a capital which had shown disrespect to monarchy.

The ancient palace of the Louvre was not fine enough for Louis, and Versailles was built at a cost of twenty millions, and at a sacrifice of many humble lives, for the labourers died at their work and were borne from the beautiful park with some attempt at secrecy. It was a stately place, and thither every courtier must hasten if he wished for the favour of the King. It became the centre of the gayest world of Europe, for there were ambassadors there from every foreign court.

Etiquette, so wearisome to many monarchs, was the delight of the punctilious Louis XIV; every detail of his life was carried out with due regard to the dignity that he held to be the fitting appendage of a king. When he rose and dressed, when he dined or gave audience, there were fixed rules to be observed. He was never alone though he built Marly, expressing some wish that he might retire occasionally from the weariness of the court routine. His brothers stood in the royal presence, and there was no real family life. He was the grand monarch, and represented the majesty of France most worthily on the occasions of ceremony, when velvet and diamonds increased his stately grace. "The State—it is Myself," he was fond of declaring, and by this remark satisfied his conscience when he levied exorbitant taxes to support the lavish magnificence of his court.

Ignorant as the king was through the device of Mazarin, he was proud of the genius that shed lustre on the French nation. Corneille and Racine wrote tragedies of classic fame, and Molière, the greatest of all comedians, could amuse the wit of every visitor to the court. Louis gave banquets at Versailles in honour of the dramatists he patronized, and had their plays performed in a setting so brilliant that ambition might well be satisfied. Tales of royal bounty spread afar and attracted the needy genius of other lands. Louis' heart swelled with pride when he received the homage of the learned and beheld the deference of messengers from less splendid courts. He sat on a silver throne amid a throng of nobles he had stripped of power. It was part of his policy to bring every landowner to Versailles, where fortunes vanished rapidly. It was useless to hope for office if the suitor did not come to make a personal appeal.

Parisians grumbled that the capital should be deserted by the King, but they were appeased on holidays by free admission to the sights of sumptuous Versailles. The King himself would occasionally appear in ballets performed by some exclusive company of the court. There was always feasting toward and sweet music composed by Lulli, and they were amazed and interested by the dazzling jets of water from the fountains that had cost such fabulous sums. Court beauties were admired together with the Guards surrounding the King's person in such fine array. Rumours of the countless servants attached to the service of the court gave an impression that the power of France could never fail. Patriotic spirit was aroused by the fine spectacle of the hunting-train as it rode toward the forests which lay between Versailles and the capital. The Grand Huntsman of France was a nobleman, and had a splendid retinue. "*Hallali, valets! Hallali!*" was echoed by many humble sportsmen when the stag was torn to pieces by the pack.

A special stud of horses was reserved for Louis' use in time of war. He had shown himself a bold youth on the battlefield in Mazarin's time, fighting in the trenches like a common soldier that his equipment might not be too heavy an expense. He chose, however, to be magnificent enough as a warrior when he disturbed the peace of Europe by his arrogant pride.

Philip IV of Spain died in 1665, leaving his dominions to Charles II, half-brother of France's Queen. Louis declared that Maria Theresa had not been of age when she renounced her claims and that, moreover, the dowry of 500,000 golden crowns promised in consideration

of this renunciation had not been paid. He wished to
secure to his consort the Flemish provinces of Brabant,
Mechlin, Antwerp, etc., and to this end made a treaty
with the Dutch. He was compelled to postpone his
attack on the Spanish possessions by a war with England
which broke out through his alliance with Holland,
her great commercial rival at that date.

Louis XIV showed himself perfidious in his relation-
ship with the Dutch when he concluded a secret peace
with Charles II of England in 1667. He marched into
the Netherlands, supported by a new alliance with
Portugal, and intended to claim the whole Spanish
monarchy at some future date. Many towns surrendered,
for he had a well-disciplined army and no lack of personal
courage. Turenne and Condé, his brave generals, made
rapid conquests which filled all Europe with alarm.

But Louis' campaigns involved him in disastrous
warfare with too many foes. He was a bigoted persecutor of the Protestant, and made a secret treaty with
England's treacherous ruler, Charles II, who, to his
lasting shame, became a pensioner of the French King,
agreeing, in return for French subsidies, to second Louis'
designs on Spain. France herself was torn by wars of
religion in 1698 when the Edict of Nantes was revoked
and the real intentions of the King were revealed to
subjects who had striven, in the face of persecution, to
be loyal.

Louis XIV was under the influence of Madame de
Maintenon, whom he married privately after the death
of his neglected Queen. This favourite, once the royal
governess and widow of the poet Scarron, was strictly
pious, and desired to see the Protestants conform. She
founded the convent of Saint-Cyr, a place of education
for beautiful young orphan girls, and placed at the head

of it Fénélon, the priest and writer. She urged the King continually to suppress heresy in his dominions, and was gratified by the sudden and deadly persecution that took place as the seventeenth century closed.

Torture and death were excused as acts necessary for the establishment of the true faith, and soon all France was hideous with scenes of martyrdom. Children were dragged from their parents and placed in Catholic households, where their treatment was most cruel unless they promised to embrace the Catholic religion. Women suffered every kind of indignity at the hands of the soldiers who were sent to live in the houses and at the cost of heretics. These *Dragonnades* were carried on with great brutality, shameful carousals being held in homes once distinguished for elegance and refinement. Nuns had instructions to convert the novices under their rule by any means they liked to employ. Some did not hesitate to obtain followers of the Catholic Church by the use of the scourge, and fasting and imprisonment in noisome dungeons.

There was fierce resistance in the country districts, and armed men sprang up to defend their homes, welcoming even civil war if by that means they could attain protection. The contest was unequal, for the peasants had been weakened by centuries of oppression, and there were strange seignorial rights which the weak dared not refuse when they were opposing the government in their obstinate choice of a religion.

The reign of the Grand Monarch was losing radiance, though Louis was far from acknowledging that all was not well in that broad realm which owned him master. He had discarded the frivolities of his youth and kept a dreary solemn state at Versailles, where decorous Madame de Maintenon was all-powerful. He did not lament his Spanish wife nor Colbert the minister, who died in the same year, for strict integrity was not valued too highly by the King of France. Yet Colbert's work remained in the mighty palaces his constructive energy had planned, the bridges and fortresses and factories which he had held necessary for France's future greatness as a nation. Louis paid scant tribute of regret to the memory of one who had toiled indefatigably in his service; but he looked complacently on Versailles and reflected that it would survive, even if the laurels of glory should be wrested from his brow.

In 1700, Louis' prestige had dwindled in Europe, where he had once been feared as a sovereign ambitious for universal monarchy. William the Stadtholder, now ruler of England with his Stuart wife, had been disgusted by the persecution of the French Protestants and had resolved to avenge Louis' seizure of his principality of Orange. Chance enabled this man to ally the greater part of Europe against the ambition of the Grand Monarch. War had been declared by England against France in 1689, and prosecuted most vigorously till Louis XIV was gradually deprived of his finest conquests. Though this was concluded in 1697 by the Peace of Ryswick, the French King's attempt to win the crown of Spain for his grandson, the Duke of Anjou, caused a renewal of hostilities.

William III was in failing health, but a mighty general had arisen to defeat the projects of the French King. The news of the Duke of Marlborough's victories in Flanders made it evident that the power of Louis XIV in the battlefield was waning. Yet the French monarch did not reflect the terror on the faces of his courtiers when the great defeat of Lille was announced in his royal palace. He observed all the usual duties of his daily life and affected a serenity that other men might envy when they bewailed the passing of the Old Order, or repeated the prophecy once made by an astrologer that the end of Louis XIV's reign should not be glorious as the beginning.

The King retained his marvellous composure to the last, too haughty to bend before misfortune or to retire even if the enemy came to the very gates of Paris. At seventy-six he still went out to hunt the stag; he held Councils of State long after his health was really broken. He said farewell to the officers of the crown in a voice as strong as ever when he was banished to the sick-room in 1715, and upbraided the weeping attendants, asking them if they had indeed come to consider him immortal.

The reign of seventy-two years, so memorable in the annals of France, drew to a close with the life that had embodied all its royalty. Louis XIV died " as a candle that goes out "—deserted even by Madame de Maintenon, who determined to secure herself against adversity by retirement to the convent of Saint-Cyr. There was no loud mourning as the King's corpse was driven to the tomb on a car of black and silver, for the new century knew not the old reverence for kings. It was the age of Voltaire and the mocking sceptic.

Chapter XII

Peter the Great

ON the very day when the Grand Monarch watched his army cross the Rhine under the generals—Turenne and Condé—a man was born possessed of the same strong individuality as Louis XIV, a man whose rule was destined to work vast changes in the mighty realms to the extreme east of Europe.

On 30th May, 1672, Peter, son of Alexis, was born in the palace of the Kreml at Moscow. He was reared at first in strict seclusion behind the silken curtains that guarded the windows of the *Térem*, where the women lived. Then rebellion broke out after his father's death; for Alexis had children by two marriages, and the offspring of his first wife, Mary Miloslavski, were jealous of the influence acquired by the relatives of Nathalie Naryshkin, Peter's mother.

Peter found a strange new freedom in the village near Moscow which gave him shelter when the Miloslavski were predominant in the State. He grew up wild and boisterous, the antithesis in all things of the polished courtier of the western world, for he despised fine clothing and hated the external pomp of state. He ruled at first with his half-brother Ivan, and had reason to dread the power of Ivan's sister, Sophia Miloslavski, who was Regent, and gave lavish emoluments to Galitzin, her favourite minister. There was even an attempt upon Peter's life, which made him something of a coward in later times, since he was taken unawares by a terrible rising that Sophia inspired and escaped her only by a hurried flight.

The rising was put down, however; Sophia was sent to a convent, and Galitzin banished before Peter could be said to rule. He did not care at first for State affairs, being absorbed by youthful pleasures which he shared with companions from the stables and the streets. He drilled soldiers, forming pleasure regiments, and had hours of delight sailing an old boat which he found one day, for this aroused a new enthusiasm. There were Dutch skippers at Archangel who were glad to teach him all they knew of navigation and the duties of their various crafts. The Tsar insisted on working his way upward from a cabin-boy—he was democratic, and intended to level classes in his Empire in this way.

Russian subjects complained bitterly of the Tsar's strange foreign tastes as soon as they heard that he was fond of visiting the *Sloboda*, that German quarter of his capital where so many foreigners lived. There were rumours that he was not Alexis' son but the offspring perhaps of Lefort, the Genevese favourite, who helped him to reform. When it was reported that he was about to visit foreign lands, discontent was louder, for the rulers of the east did not travel far from their own dominions if they followed the customs of their fathers, and observed their people's will. The *Streltsy*, a privileged class of soldiers, rose on the eve of the departure for the west. Their punishment did not descend on them at once, but Peter planned a dark vengeance in his mind.

The monarch visited many countries in disguise, intent on learning the civilized arts of western Europe, that he might introduce them to " barbarous Muscovy," which clung to the obsolete practices of a former age. He spent some time at Zaandem, a village in Holland, where he was busily engaged in boat-building. Then he was entertained at Amsterdam, and passed on to England as the guest of William III. He occupied Sayes Court, near Deptford, the residence of John Evelyn, the great diarist, and wrought much havoc in that pleasant place; for his manners were still rude and barbarous, and he had no respect for the property of his host. Sir Godfrey Kneller painted him—a handsome giant, six feet eight inches high, with full lips, dark skin, and curly hair that always showed beneath his wig. The Tsar disdained to adorn his person, and was often meanly clad, wearing coarse darned stockings, thick shoes, and studying economy in dress.

Peter continued his study of ship-building at Deptford, but the chief object of his visit was fulfilled when he had induced workmen of all kinds to return with him to Russia to teach their different trades. The Tsar was intent on securing a fleet, and hoped to gain a sea-board for his empire by driving back the Poles and Swedes from their Baltic ports. He would then be able to trade with Europe and have intercourse with countries that were previously unknown. But only war could accomplish this high ambition, and he had, as yet, no real skill in arms. An attempt on Azov, then in Turkish hands, had led to ignominious defeat.

Peter returned home to find that the *Streltsy* had broken out again. His vengeance was terrible, for he had a barbarous strain and wielded the axe and knout with his own hands. The rebellious soldiers were deprived of the privileges that had long been theirs, and those who were fortunate enough to escape a cruel death were banished. In future the army was to know the discipline that such soldiers as Patrick Gordon, a Scotch officer, had learned in their campaigns in foreign lands. This soldier did much good work in the organization and control of Peter's army. Their dress was to be modelled on the western uniforms that Peter had admired. He was ashamed of the cumbersome skirts that Russians wore after the Asiatic style, and insisted that they should be cut off, together with the beards that were almost sacred in the eyes of priests.

Favourites of humble origin were useful to Peter in his innovations, which were rigorously carried out. Menshikof, once a pastry-cook's boy, aided the Tsar to crush any discontent that might break out, and himself shaved many wrathful nobles who were afraid to resist. It was Peter's whim to give such lavish presents to this minister that he could live in splendid luxury and entertain the Tsar's own guests. Peter himself preferred simplicity, and despised the magnificence of fine palaces. He married a serving-maid named Catherine for his second wife, and loved her homely household ways and the cheerful spirit with which she rode out with him to camp. His first wife was shut up in a convent because she had a sincere distrust of all the changes that began with Peter's reign.

Charles XII of Sweden was the monarch who had chief reason to beware of the impatient spirit of the Tsar, ever desirous of that "window open upon Europe," which his father too had craved. The Swede was warlike and fearless, for he was happy only in the field. He scorned Peter's claims at first, and inflicted shameful defeat on him. The Tsar fled from Narva in Livonia, and all Europe branded him as coward. By 1700, peace with Turkey had been signed in order that the

Russians might march westward to the Baltic sea. Their repulse showed the determination of the Tsar, who had learnt a lesson from the humiliation he had endured. He began to train soldiers and sailors again, and sent for more foreigners to teach the art of war. The very church-bells were melted into cannon-balls that he might conquer the all-conquering Swedes.

Moscow, which consisted largely of wooden buildings, caught fire and was burnt in 1701, both palace and state offices falling to the ground. The capital had dreadful memories for the Tsar, who wished to build a new fort looking out upon the Baltic Sea. Its ancient churches and convents did not attract him, for religion was strongly associated in his mind with the stubborn opposition of the priesthood, which invariably met his plans for reform.

Petersburg rose in triumph on an island of the Neva when the estuary had been seized by a superb effort of the Tsar. It was on a damp unhealthy site and contained only wooden huts in its first period of occupation, but inhabitants were quickly found. The Tsar was autocratic enough to bid his *boyards*, or nobles, move there despite all their complaints. He built the church of St Peter and St Paul, and drew merchants thither by promises of trade. "Let him build towns," his adversary said with scorn, "there will be all the more for us to take."

The King of Poland had allied himself with Russia against Sweden, but proved faithless and unscrupulous as the contest waxed keen. Augustus had found some qualities in the Tsar which appealed to him, for he was boisterous in mirth himself and a hard drinker, but his principal concern was for the safety of his own throne and the security of his own dominions. After two decisive defeats, he was expelled from the throne of Poland by Charles XII, who placed Stanislaus Leszczynski in his place. This alarmed Peter, who had relied on Poland's help. The winter and cold proved a better ally of Russia in the end than any service which Augustus paid. The Tsar wisely drew the Swedish army into the desert-lands, where many thousands died of cold and hunger. He met the forlorn remnants of a glorious band at Poltava in 1709, and routed them with ease. Narva was avenged, for the Swedish King had to be led from the battlefield by devoted comrades and placed in retreat in Turkey, where he was the Sultan's guest. Charles' lucky star had set when he received a wound the night before Poltava, for he could not fight on foot and his men lost heart, missing the stern heroic figure and the commanding voice that bade them gain either victory or death.

Peter might well order an annual celebration of his victory over Sweden, writing exultantly to Admiral Apraxin at Petersburg some few hours after battle, "Our enemy has encountered the fate of Phaethon, and the foundation-stone of our city on the Neva is at length grimly laid." The Swedish army had been crushed, and the Swedish hero-king was a mere knight-errant unable to return to his own land. The Cossacks who had tried to assert their independence of Russia under the Hetman Mazeppa, an ally of Charles XII, failed in their opposition to the mighty Tsar. Augustus was recognized as King of Poland again after the defeat of the Swedish King at Poltava, as Stanislaus retired, knowing that he could expect no further support from Sweden. Peter renewed his alliance at Thorn with the Polish sovereign.

The new order began for Russia as soon as the Baltic coast fell into the possession of Peter, who was overjoyed by the new link with the west. He was despotic in his sweeping changes, but he desired the civilization of his barbarous land. He visited foreign courts, disliking their ceremony and half-ashamed of his homely faithful wife. He gathered new knowledge everywhere, learning many trades and acquiring treasures that were the gifts of kings. It was long before his ambassadors were respected, longer still before he received the ungrudging acknowledgment of his claims as Emperor. He had resolved to form great alliances through his daughters, who were educated and dressed after the manner of the French.

Peter did much for the emancipation of women in Russia, though his personal treatment of them was brutal, and he threatened even Catherine with death if she hesitated to obey his slightest whim. They had been reared in monotonous retirement hitherto, and never saw their bridegrooms till the marriage-day. Their wrongs were seldom redressed if they ventured to complain, and the convent was the only refuge from unhappy married life. The royal princesses were not allowed to appear in public nor drive unveiled through the streets. Suitors did not release them from the dreary empty routine of their life, because their religion was a barrier to alliance with princes of the west. Sophia had dared greatly in demanding a position in the State.

Peter altered the betrothal customs, insisting that the bridal couple should meet before the actual ceremonies took place. He gave assemblies to which his subjects were obliged by *ukase* or edict to bring the women of their families, and he endeavoured to promote that social life which had been unknown in Russia when she was cut off from the west. He approved of dancing and music, and took part in revels of a more boisterous kind. He drank very heavily in his later days, and was peremptory in bidding both men and women share the convivial pleasures of his court. National feeling was suspicious of all feminine influence till the affable Catherine entered public life. She interceded for culprits, and could often calm her husband in his most violent moods. Gradually the attitude changed which had made proverbs expressing such sentiments as " A woman's hair is long, but her understanding is short."

Peter's fierce impetuous nature bore the nation along the new channel in which he chose that it should flow. He played at being a servant, but he made use of the supreme authority of an Emperor. All men became absorbed in his strong imperious personality which differed from the general character of the Russian of his day. Relentless severity marked his displeasure when any disaffection was likely to thwart his favourite plans. He sacrificed his eldest son Alexis to this theory that every man must share his tastes. " The knout is not an angel, but it teaches men to tell the truth," he said grimly, as he examined the guilty by torture and drew confession with the lash.

St Petersburg became the residence of the nobles. They had to desert their old estates and follow the dictates of a Tsar whose object it was to push continually toward the west. Labourers died in thousands while the city was built and destroyed again by winter floods, but the past for Russia was divided from the future utterly at Peter's death in 1725.

Chapter XIII

The Royal Robber

PETER THE GREAT had paid a famous visit to the Prussian court, hoping to conclude an alliance with Frederick William I against Charles XII, his northern adversary. Queen Catherine and her ladies had been sharply criticized when they arrived at Berlin, and Peter's own bearing did not escape much adverse comment and secret ridicule; nevertheless he received many splendid presents, and these, no doubt, atoned to him for anything which seemed lacking in his reception.

A splendid yacht sailed toward Petersburg as the gift of Frederick, who was anxious to conciliate the uncouth ruler of the East. In return, men of gigantic stature were sent annually from Russia to enter the splendid Potsdam Guards, so dear to the monarch, who was a stern soldier and loved the martial life. Prussia was a new kingdom obtained for his descendants by the Elector of Brandenburg. It was necessary that the rulers should devote themselves to recruiting a goodly force, since their land might be easily attacked by foreign foes and divided among the greater powers, if they did not protect it well.

Frederick William sent recruiting sergeants far and wide, and suffered these even to enter churches during service and to carry off by force the stalwart young men of the congregation. Yet he was a pious man, an enemy to vice, and a ruler of enormous diligence. He rid himself of useless attendants as soon as his father died, and exercised the strictest economy in his private life. He kept the purse-strings and was also his own general. He was ever about the streets, accosting idlers roughly, and bidding the very apple-women knit at their stalls while they were awaiting custom. He preached industry everywhere, and drilled his regiments with zealous assiduity.

Of tall stature and florid complexion, the King struck terror into the hearts of the coward and miscreant. He despised extravagance in dress. French foppery was so hateful to him that he clothed the prison gaolers in Parisian style, trusting that this would bring contempt on foreign fashions.

The Potsdam Guards were under the strictest discipline, and the Prussian soldiers won battles by sheer mechanical obedience to orders when they took the field. Death punished any resistance to a superior officer, and merciless flogging was inflicted on the rank and file. Boys were often reluctant to enter on such a course of training, and parents were compelled to give up their sons by means of *Dragonnades*—soldiers quartered upon subjects who were not sufficiently patriotic to furnish recruits for the State. Every man of noble birth had to be an officer, and must serve until his strength was broken. The King fraternized only with soldiers because these were above other classes and belonged more or less to his own order. The army had been raised to 80,000 men when Frederick William I died, holding the fond belief that his successor had it in his power to enlarge the little kingdom which the old Elector had handed down with pride.

The Royal Robber

The Crown Prince, Frederick of Brandenburg and Hohenzollern, was born in the royal palace of Berlin on January 24th of 1712. He was christened Friedrich —" rich in peace "—a name strangely ironical since he was trained from his earliest years to adopt a martial life. From the child's eighth year he was educated by military tutors, and bred in simple habits that would make him able to endure the hardships of a camp.

The martinet, Frederick William I, laid down strict rules for his son's training, for he longed to be followed by a lad of military tastes. He was to learn no Latin but to study Arithmetic, Mathematics and Artillery and to be thoroughly instructed in Economy. The fear of God was to be impressed on the pupil, and prayers and Church services played an important part in the prince's day, of which every hour had its allotted task. Haste and cleanliness were inculcated in the simple royal toilette, for Frederick I had, for those days, a quite exaggerated idea of cleanliness, but he particularly impressed upon attendants that "Prayer with washing, breakfast and the rest" were to be performed within fifteen minutes. It was a hard life, destined to bring the boy a "true love for the soldier business." He was commanded to love it and seek in it his sole glory. The father returned from war with the Swedes in January 1716, victorious, and delighted to see the little Fritz, then of the tender age of three, beating a toy drum, and his sister Wilhelmina, aged seven, in a martial attitude.

But the Crown Prince began to disappoint his father by playing the flute and reading French romances. He liked fine clothes too, and was caught wearing a richly embroidered dressing-gown, to the rage of the King, who put it in the fire. Frederick liked to arrange his hair in flowing locks instead of in a club after the military fashion. "A *Querpfeifer und Poet*, not a soldier," the indignant father growled, believing the *Querpfeif*, or Cross-Pipe, was only fit for a player in the regimental band. Augustus William, another son, ten years younger than Fritz, began to be the hope of parental ambition. He took more kindly to a Spartan life than his elder brother. There were violent scenes at court when Frederick the younger was asked to give up his right to the succession. He refused to be superseded, and had to endure much bullying and privation. The King was ever ready with his stick, and punished his son by omitting to serve him at his rather scanty table !

There was much talk of a double marriage between the English and the Prussian courts, which were then related. Frederick was to marry Amelia, daughter of George I while his sister, pretty pert Wilhelmina, was destined for Frederick, Prince of Wales. The King of Prussia set his heart on the plan, and was furious that George I did not forward it. The whole household went in fear of him; he was stricken by gout at the time, an affliction that made him particularly ill-tempered, and Wilhelmina and Fritz were the objects of his wrath. They fled from his presence together; the Prince was accused of a dissolute life, and insulted by a beating in public.

He decided on flight to England. It was a desperate measure, and was discovered and frustrated at the last moment. The King of Prussia laid the blame on English diplomats, though they had done nothing to help the Prince. There was talk of an Austro-English war at that time. " I shall not desert the Emperor even if everything goes to the dogs," wrote the irate father. " I will joyfully use my army, my country, my money and my blood for the downfall of England." He was so enraged by the attempted flight that he might have gone to the extreme of putting his son to death, but an old general, hearing of the probable fate of the Crown Prince, offered his own life for that of Frederick, and raised so vehement a protest that the runaway was merely put in prison.

His confinement was not as strict as it would have been, had the gaolers followed the King's orders. He had to wear prison dress and sit on a hard stool, but books and writing materials were brought to him, and he saw his friends occasionally. Lieutenant von Katte, who fled with him, was executed before the fortress, and the Prince was compelled to witness the punishment of the companion with whom he had practised music and other forbidden occupations.

By degrees, the animosity of Frederick William toward his eldest son softened. He was allowed to visit Berlin when his sister Wilhelmina was married to the Margrave of Baireuth, after four kings had applied for her hand, among them the elderly Augustus of Poland and Charles XII of Sweden. The Castle of Rheinsburg, near Neu-Ruppin, was given to the Prince for his residence. He spent happy hours there with famous men of letters in his circle, for he was actually free now to give time to literature and science. He corresponded frequently with Voltaire and became an atheist. He cared nothing for religion when he was king, and was remarkable for the religious toleration which he extended to his subjects. But the harsh treatment of youth had spoilt his pleasant nature, and his want of faith made him unscrupulous and hard-hearted. He grasped at all he could win, and had every intention of fulfilling the commands laid upon him by the Testament which his father wrote in 1722 when he believed himself to be dying:—"Never relinquish what is justly yours."

It was far from his intention to relinquish any part of his dominions, and, moreover, he set early about the business of conquering Silesia to add to his little kingdom. Saxony should fall to him if he could in any wise win it. There was hope in that fine stalwart body of men his father had so well disciplined. There was courage in his own heart, and he had been reared in too stern a school to fear hardships.

In 1740, Frederick received his dying father's blessing, and in the same year the Emperor, Charles VI, left his daughter, Maria Theresa, to struggle with an aggressive European neighbour. She was a splendid figure, this empress of twenty-three, beautiful and virtuous, with the spirit of a man, and an unconquerable determination to fight for what was justly hers. She held not Austria alone but many neighbouring kingdoms—Styria, Bohemia, the Tyrol, Hungary, and Carpathia

Charles VI had endeavoured to secure his daughter's kingdom by means of a "Pragmatic Sanction," which declared the indivisibility of the Austrian dominions, and the right of Maria Theresa to inherit them in default of a male heir. This was signed by all the powers of Europe save Bavaria, but Frederick broke it ruthlessly as soon as the Emperor died.

In high spirits Frederick II entered on the bold enterprise of seizing from Maria Theresa some part of those possessions which her father had striven to secure to her.

Allies gathered round Prussia quickly, admiring the 80,000 men that the obscure sovereignty had raised from the subjects of a little kingdom. France, Spain, Poland, and Bavaria allied themselves with the spoiler against Maria Theresa, who sought the aid of England. She

The Royal Robber

seemed in desperate straits, the victim of treachery, for Frederick had promised to support her. The Battle of Molwitz went against Austria, and the Empress was fain to offer three duchies of Silesia, but the King refused them scornfully, saying, " Before the war, they might have contented me. Now I want more. What do I care about peace ? Let those who want it give me what I want ; if not, let them fight me and be beaten again."

The Elector of Bavaria was within three days' march of Vienna, proclaiming himself Archduke of Austria. Maria Theresa had neither men nor money. Quite suddenly she took a resolution and convoked the Hungarian magnates at Pressburg, where she had fled from her capital. She stood before them, most beautiful and patriotic in her youth and helplessness. Raising her baby in her arms, she appealed to the whole assembly. She had put on the crown of St Stephen and held his sword at her side. The appeal was quickly answered. Swords leapt from their scabbards ; there came the roar of many voices, " *Moriamur pro rege nostro, Maria Theresa!* " (" Let us die for our King, Maria Theresa.")

But Friedrich defeated the Austrians again and again in battle. No armies could resist those wonderful compact regiments, perfectly drilled and disciplined, afraid of nothing save of losing credit. Maria had to submit to the humiliation of giving up part of Silesia to her enemy, while the Elector had himself crowned as Emperor Charles VII at Frankfort. The English King, George II, fought for her against the French at Dettingen and won a victory. She entered her capital in triumph, apparently confirmed in her possessions. But Frederick was active in military operations and attempted to detach the English from her. He invaded Bohemia and defeated the imperial generals. He received the much-disputed territory of Silesia in 1745 by the Treaty of Dresden, which concluded the second war.

The national spirit was rising in Prussia through this all-powerful army, which drained the country of its men and horses. The powers of Europe saw with astonishment that a new force was arraying itself in youthful glory. The Seven Years' War began in 1756, one of the most fateful wars in the whole of European history.

France, Russia, and Saxony were allied with Maria Theresa, but the Prussians had the help of England. Frederick II proved himself a splendid general, worthy of the father whose only war had wrested the coveted province of Pomerania from the doughty Charles XII of Sweden. He defeated the Austrians and invaded Saxony, mindful of the wealth and prosperity of that country which, if added to his own, would greatly increase the value of his dominions. He was almost always victorious though he had half Europe against him. He defeated the Austrians at Prague and Leuthen, the Russian army at Zorndorf. One of his most brilliant triumphs was won over the united French and Imperial armies at Rossbach.

The French anticipated an easy victory in 1757, for the army of the allies was vastly superior to that which Frederick William had encamped at Rossbach, a village in Prussian Saxony. The King watched the movements of the enemy from a castle, and was delighted when he managed to bring them to a decisive action. He had partaken of a substantial meal with his soldiers in the camp, although he was certainly in a most precarious

Frederick the Great receiving his People's Homage
A. Menzel

The Royal Robber 153

position. He was too cunning a strategist to give the signal to his troops till the French were advancing up the hill toward his tents. The battle lasted only one hour and a half and resulted in a complete victory for Prussia. The total loss of the King's army was under 550 officers and men compared with 7700 on the side of the enemy.

The "Army of Cut-and-Run" was the contemptuous name earned by the retreating regiments.

Gradually, allies withdrew on either side, France becoming involved with England in India and the Colonies. Frederick II and Maria Theresa made terms at Hubertsburg. Silesia was still in the hands of the Prussian King, but he had failed in the prime object of the war, which was the conquest of Saxony.

There was work for a king at home when the long, disastrous war was over. Harvests went unreaped for want of men, and there were no strong horses left for farm-labour. Starvation had rendered many parts of the kingdom desolate, but the introduction of the potato saved some of those remaining. The King had forthwith to rebuild villages and bring horses from foreign countries. He was anxious to follow his father's exhortations and make the population industrious and thriving. He saw to it that schools rose everywhere and churches also, in which there was as little bickering as possible. The clergy were kept down and prevented from "becoming popes," as seemed to be the case in some countries. The King had no piety, but revered his father's Protestantism.

When the war was over, Frederick looked an old man though he was but fifty-one. He was a shabby figure, this "old Fritz," in threadbare blue uniform with red facings. His three-cornered hat, black breeches and long boots showed signs of an economical spirit, inculcated in his youth when he had only eighteen pence a week to spend. He walked about among the country people talking familiarly with the farmers. He made it a rule to go round the country once a year to see how things had prospered.

The King hated idleness, and, like the first Frederick, scolded his subjects if they were not industrious. "It is not necessary that I should live, but it is necessary that whilst I live I be busy," he would remark severely. Frugality won praise from him and he always noted it among his subjects. One day he asked the time of an officer he met in the streets and was startled to see a leaden bullet pulled up by a golden chain. "My watch points to but one hour, that in which I am ready to die for your Majesty," was the patriotic answer to his question. He rewarded the officer with his own gold watch, and reflected that his methods had been as successful as those of his father. That prudent monarch put loose sleeves over his uniform whenever he wrote that he might not spoil the expensive cloth which was then the fashion.

In 1786, Frederick II died, leaving Germany to mourn him. The best-disciplined army in Europe and a treasury full of gold were the good gifts he left to his successor. The population of the realm numbered six million souls, in itself another fortune. "If the country is thickly populated, that is true wealth" had been a wise maxim of the first Frederick.

Father and son cut homely figures on the stage of eighteenth-century Europe. The brilliant Louis XIV, and his stately Versailles, seemed to far outshine them. But Germany owed to Frederick I and Frederick II, known as the Great, her unity and national spirit.

They built on solid ground and their work remained to bring power to their successors, while the Grand Monarch left misery behind, which was to find expression in that crying of the oppressed, known throughout history as the French Revolution.

Chapter XIV

Spirits of the Age

IT was the aim of Frederick the Great to shake down the old political order in Europe, which had been Catholic and unenlightened. To that end he exalted Prussia, which was a Protestant and progressive State, and fought against Austria, an empire clinging to obsolete ideas of feudal military government. He brought upon himself much condemnation for his unjust partition of Poland with Russia. He argued, however, that Poland had hitherto been a barbaric feudal State, and must benefit by association with countries of commercial and intellectual activity. Galicia fell to Maria Theresa at the end of the war, and was likely to remain in religious bondage.

Frederick II dealt many hard blows at the Holy Catholic Church, but he did not intend to wage a religious war in Europe. He insisted on toleration in Prussia though he was not himself a religious man, and invited to his court that enemy of the old faith of France— François Marie Arouet, better known as Voltaire, a title he derived from the name of an estate in the possession of his family.

The French scholar came to Frederick after he had suffered every persecution that inevitably assailed a fearless writer in an age of narrow bigotry. Very soon after his appearance in Paris, Voltaire was accused of writing verses which recounted the evils of a country where magistrates used their power to levy unjust taxes, and loyal subjects were too often put in prison. As a consequence, he was thrown into the Bastille. It was quite useless to protest that he was not the author of *Je l'ai vu* ("I have seen it"). His opinions were suspected although he was but twenty-one and was under the protection of his godfather, the Abbé Châteauneuf. Voltaire was philosopher enough to use his year in the Bastille very profitably—he finished his first great tragedy, *Œdipe*, and produced it in 1716, winning the admiration of French critics.

Although Voltaire was now embarked on a brilliant career as a dramatist, he was unjustly treated by his superiors in social rank. He was the son of a notary of some repute, and was too rich to sue for patronage, but nobles were offended by the freedom of the young wit, who declared that a poet might claim equality with princes. "Who is the young man who talks so loud?" the Chevalier Rohan inquired at an intellectual gathering. "My lord," was Voltaire's quick reply, "he is one who does not bear a great name but wins respect for the name he has."

This apt retort did not please the Chevalier, who instructed his lackey to give the poet a beating. Voltaire would have answered the insult with his sword, but his enemy disdained a duel with a man of inferior station. The Rohan family was influential, and preferred to maintain their dignity by putting the despised poet in prison.

Voltaire was ordered to leave Paris and decided to visit England, where he knew that learned Frenchmen found a welcome. He was amazed at the high honour paid to genius and the social and political consequence which could be obtained by writers. Jonathan Swift, the famous Irish satirist, was a dignitary of the State Church and yet never hesitated to heap scorn on State abuses. Addison, the classical scholar, was Secretary of State, and Prior and Gay went on important diplomatic missions. Philosophers, such as Newton and Locke, had wealth as well as much respect, and were entrusted with a share in the administration of their country. With his late experience of French injustice, Voltaire may have been inclined to exaggerate the absolute freedom of an English subject to handle public events and public personages in print. "One must disguise at Paris what I could not say too strongly at London," he wrote, and the hatred quickened in him of all forms of class prejudice and intellectual obstinacy.

His *Lettres anglaises*, which moved many social writers of his time, were burnt in public by the decree of the Parlement of Paris in 1734. The Parlement, composed of men of the robe (lawyers), was closely allied to the court in narrow-minded bigotry. It was always to the fore to prevent any manifestation of free thought from reaching the people. The old order, clinging to wealth and favour, judged it best that the people—known as the Third Estate—should remain in ignorance of the enormous oppressions put upon them. It had been something of a shock to Voltaire to discover that in England both nobles and clergy paid taxes, while in France the saying of feudal times held good—"The nobles fight, the clergy pray, the people pay."

Sadly wanting in respect to those in high places was that Voltaire who had not long ago been beaten by a noble's lackeys. He did not cease to write, and continued to give offence, though the sun of the court shone on him once through Madame de Pompadour, the King's favourite. She caused him to write a play

Spirits of the Age

in 1745 to celebrate the marriage of the Dauphin. The *Princesse de Navarre* brought him more honour than had been accorded to his finest poems and tragedies. He was admitted to the Academy of Letters which Richelieu had founded, made Gentleman of the Chamber, and Historiographer of France.

It was well in those times to write for royal favour, though the subjects of the drama must be limited to those which would add glory to the Church or State. Yet Voltaire did not need the patronage which was essential for poor men of genius like the playwrights of the famous generation preceding his own. He had private means which he invested profitably, being little anxious to endure the insults commonly directed at poverty and learning. He lived in a quiet château at Cirey, industrious and independent, though he looked toward the Marquise du Châtelet for that admiration which a literary man craves. It was the Marquise who shared with Frederick the Great the tribute paid by the witty man of letters, *i.e.* that there were but two great men in his time and one of them wore petticoats. She differed from the frivolous women of court life in her earnest pursuit of intellectual pleasures. Her whole day was given up to the study of writers such as Leibnitz and Newton, the philosopher. She rarely wasted time, and could certainly claim originality in that her working hours were never broken by social interruptions. She was unamiable, but had no love for slander, though she was herself the object of much spiteful gossip from women who passed as wits in the corrupt court life of Versailles.

Voltaire came and went, moving up and down Europe, often the object of virulent attacks which made flight a necessity, but for fifteen years he returned regularly to the solitary château of Cirey, where he could depend upon seclusion for the active prosecution of his studies. He was a man with a wide range of interests, dabbling in science and performing experiments for his own profit. He wrote history, in addition to plays and poetry, and later, in his attacks upon the Church, proved himself a skilful and unscrupulous controversialist.

In 1750, Madame du Châtelet being dead, Voltaire accepted the invitation which had been sent to him from Berlin by the King of Prussia. He was installed sumptuously at Potsdam, where the court of Frederick the Great was situated. There he could live in familiar intercourse with "the king who had won five battles." He loved to take an active part in life, and moved from one place to another, showing a keen interest in novelty, although his movements might also be inspired by fear of the merciless actions of the government.

At Potsdam he found activity, but not activity of intellect. Frederick the Great was drilling soldiers and received him into a stern barracks. There was a commendable toleration for free speech in the country, but there was constant bickering. At court, Voltaire found his life troubled by the intrigues of the envious courtiers, by the unreasonable vanity of the King, and the almost mediæval state of manners. There were quarrels soon between the King and his guest, which led to exhibitions of paltriness and parsimony common to their characters. The King stopped Voltaire's supply of chocolate and sugar, while Voltaire pocketed candle-ends to show his contempt for this meanness! The saying of Frederick that the Frenchman was only an orange, of which, having squeezed the juice, he should throw away the skin, very naturally rankled in the poet to whom it was repeated.

There was jealousy and tale-bearing at Potsdam which went far to destroy the mutual admiration of those two strong personalities who had thought to dwell so happily together. Voltaire spoke disparagingly of Frederick's literary achievements, and compared the task of correcting his host's French verses with that of washing dirty linen. Politeness had worn very thin when the writer described the monarch as an ape who ought to be flogged for his tricks, and gave him the nickname of *Luc*, a pet monkey which was noted for a vicious habit of biting!

In March 1753, Voltaire left the court, thoroughly weary of life in a place where there was so little interest in letters. He had a *fracas* at Frankfort, where he was required to give up the court decorations he had worn with childlike enjoyment, and also a volume of royal verses which Frederick did not wish to be made public. For five weeks he lay in prison with his niece, Madame Denis, complaining of frightful indignities. He boxed the ears of a bookseller to whom he owed money, attempted to shoot a clerk, and in general committed many strange follies which were quite opposed to his claims to philosophy. There was an end of close friendship with Prussia, but he still drew his pension and corresponded with the cynical Frederick, only occasionally referring to their notorious differences. In dispraise of the niece Madame Denis, the King abandoned the toleration he had professedly extended. "Consider all that as done with," he wrote on the subject of the imprisonment, "and never let me hear again of that wearisome niece, who has not as much merit as her uncle with which to cover her defects. People talk of the servant of Molière, but nobody will ever speak of the niece of Voltaire."

The poet resented this contempt of his niece, for he was indulgently fond of the homely coquette who was without either wit or the good sense to win pardon for the frivolity of her tastes and extravagances. Living in a learned circle, she talked, like a parrot, of literature and wrote plays for the theatre of Ferney. " She wrote a comedy; but the players, out of respect to Voltaire, declined to act in it. She wrote a tragedy; but the one favour, which the repeated entreaties of years could never wring from Voltaire, was that he would read it."

In spite of his quarrels, Voltaire spoke favourably of the German freedom which allowed writings to be published reflecting on the Great Elector. He could not endure the hostile temper of his own land and deserted Paris to settle at Geneva, that free republic which extended hospitality to refugees from all countries. He built two hermitages, one for summer and one for winter, both commanding beautiful scenes, which he enjoyed for twenty years to come, though he was not content with one shelter. He bought a life-interest in Tournay and the lordship of Ferney in 1758, declaring that " philosophers ought to have two or three holes underground against the hounds who chase them." From Ferney he denounced the religion of the time, accusing the Church of hatred of truth and real knowledge, with which was coupled a terrible cruelty and lack of toleration.

To make superstition ridiculous was one of the objects of Voltaire's satire, for, in this way, he hoped to secure due respect for reason. All abuses were to be torn away, and such traditions as made slaves of the

Spirits of the Age

people. The shameful struggles between Jesuits and Jansenists were at their height. How could religion exist when one party believing in works denied the creed of a second believing grace better than deeds, and when both sides were eager to devote themselves to persecution?

In Voltaire's day, the condemnation of free writing came chiefly from the clergy. They would shackle the mind and bring it in subjection to the priesthood. Here was a man sneering at the power claimed by members of a holy body. The narrow bigotry of priests demanded that he should be held in bondage. Yet he did not mock at men who held good lives but at the corrupt who shamed their calling. The horrors of the Inquisition were being revived by zealous Jesuits who were losing authority through the increasing strength of another party of the Catholic Church, then known as Jansenists.

The Jansenists followed the doctrines of Calvin in their belief in predestination and the necessity for conversion, but they differed widely from the Protestants on many points, holding that a man's soul was not saved directly he was converted although conversion might be instantaneous. They were firmly convinced that each human soul should have personal relation with its Maker, but held that this was only possible through the Roman Church. Their chief cause of quarrel with the Jesuits was the accusation brought against the priests of that order that they granted absolution for sins much too readily and without being certain of the sinners' real repentance.

Voltaire's blood boiled when he heard that three young Protestants had been killed because they took up arms at the sound of the tocsin, thinking it was the signal for rebellion. He received under his protection at Geneva the widow and children of the Protestant Calas, who had been broken on the wheel in 1762 because he was falsely declared to have killed his son in order to prevent his turning Catholic. A youth, named La Barre, was sentenced, at the instance of a bishop, to have his tongue and right hand cut off because he was suspected of having tampered with a crucifix. He was condemned to death afterwards on the most flimsy evidence.

Voltaire was all aflame at the ignorance of such fanatics. There was laughter in the writings of the unbelievers of the time, but it was laughter inspired by the miserable belief that jesting was the only means of enduring that which might come. "Witty things do not go well with massacres," Voltaire commented. There was force in him to destroy, and he set about destruction.

The clergy had refused in 1750 to bear their share of taxation, though one-fifth of France was in their hands. Superstition inevitably tends to make bad citizens, the philosopher observed, and set forth the evils to society that resulted from the idle lives which were supported by the labour of more industrious subjects. But in his praiseworthy attack upon the spirit of the Catholicism of his day which stooped to basest cruelty, Voltaire appealed always to intelligence rather than to feeling. He wanted to free the understanding and extend knowledge. He set up reason as a goddess, and left it to another man to point the way to a social revolution.

Jean-Jacques Rousseau it was who led men to consider the possibility of a State in which all citizens should be free and equal. He suffered banishment and much hardship for the bold schemes he presented. The Parlement of Paris was ruthless when the two books—*Émile* and the *Social Contract*—were published in 1762.

Rousseau, a writer of humble origin, had been the close student of Voltaire since his mind had first formed into a definite individuality. He had been poor and almost starving many times, had followed the occupations of engraver and music-copier, and had treated with ingratitude several kindly patrons. Like Voltaire, too, he journeyed over Europe, finding refuge in Geneva, whence came his father's family. He was a man of sordid life and without morality; but he was true to his life's purpose, and toiled at uncongenial tasks rather than write at other bidding than that of his own soul.

Rousseau's play *Le Devin du Village* had a court success that brought him into favour with gay ladies. Many a beauty found it difficult to tear herself away from the perusal of his strangely romantic novel *La Nouvelle Héloïse*, which preached a return to Nature, so long neglected by the artificial age of Paris. All conventions should be thrown off that man might attain the purity which God had originally intended. Kings there should not be to deprive their subjects of all liberty, nor nobles who claimed the earth, which was the inheritance of God's creatures.

At first, this theory of return to Nature pleased the ruling classes. The young King and Queen were well-meaning and kindly to the people. Louis XVI went among the poor and did something to alleviate the misery that he saw. Marie Antoinette gave up the extravagant career of fashion and spent happy hours in the rustic village of Trianon. Nobles and maids of honour played at rusticity, unconscious of the deadly blows that Jean-Jacques had aimed at them in the writings which appealed so strongly to their sentiment. There was a new belief in humanity which sent the Duchess out early in the morning to give bread to the poor, even if at evening she danced at a court which was supported in luxury by their miseries. The poet might congratulate himself on the sensation caused by ideas which sent him through an edict of Parlement into miserable banishment. He did not aim at destruction of the old order, but he depicted an ideal State and to attain that ideal State men butchered their fellows without mercy. The *Social Contract* became the textbook of the first revolutionary party, and none admired Rousseau more ardently than the ruthless wielder of tyranny who followed out the theorist's idea that in a republic it was necessary sometimes to have a dictator.

There were rival schools of thought during the lifetime of Voltaire and Rousseau. The latter was King of the Markets, destined in years to come to inspire the Convention and the Commune. Voltaire, companion of kings and eager recipient of the favours of Madame de Pompadour, had little sympathy with the author of a book in which the humble watchmaker's son flouted sovereignty and showed no skill in his handling of religion. The elder man offered the younger shelter when abuse was rained upon him; but Jean-Jacques would have none of it, and thought Geneva should have cast out the unbeliever, for Jean-Jacques was a pious man in theory and shocked by the worship of pure reason. The mad acclamations which greeted the return of Voltaire to Paris after thirty years of banishment must have echoed rather bitterly in the ears of Rousseau, who had despised salons and chosen to live apart from all society.

Chapter XV

The Man from Corsica

BORN on August 15th, 1769, Napoleon Buonaparte found himself surrounded from his first hours by all the tumult and the clash of war. Ajaccio, on the rocky island of Corsica, was his birthplace, though his family had Florentine blood. Letitia Ramolino, the mother of Napoleon, was of aristocratic Italian descent.

Corsica was no sunny dwelling-place during the infancy of this young hero, who learned to brood over the wrongs of his island-home. The Corsicans revolted fiercely against the sovereignty of Genoa, and were able to resist all efforts to subdue them until France interfered in the struggle and gained by diplomatic cunning what could not be gained by mere force of arms. This conquest was resented the more bitterly by the Corsicans because they had enjoyed thirteen years of independence in all but name under Paoli, a well-loved patriot. It was after Paoli was driven to England that the young Napoleon wrote, "I was born when my country was perishing, thirty thousand Frenchmen vomited upon our coasts, drowning the throne of Liberty in waves of blood; such was the sight which struck my eyes."

Corsican Napoleon declared himself in the youth of poverty and discontent, when he had dreams of rising to power by such patriotism as had ennobled Paoli. Charles Buonaparte, his father, went over to the winning side, and was eager to secure the friendship of Marbœuf, the French governor of Corsica.

Napoleon, the second of thirteen children, owed assistance in his early education to Marbœuf for it was impossible for his own family to do more than provide the barest necessities of life. Charles Buonaparte was an idle, careless man and the family poverty bore hardly on his wife Letitia, who had been married at fifteen and compelled to perform much drudgery.

Napoleon entered the military school at Brienne in April 1779, and from there sent letters which might well have warned his parents that they had hatched a prodigy. All the bitterness of a proud humiliated spirit inspired them, whether the boy, despised by richer students, begged his father to remove him, or urged, with utter disregard of filial piety, the repayment by some means of a sum of money he had borrowed.

"If I am not to be allowed the means, either by you or my protector, to keep up a more honourable appearance at the school I am in, send for me home and that immediately. I am quite disgusted with being looked upon as a pauper by my insolent companions, who have only fortune to recommend them, and smile at my poverty; there is not one here, but who is far inferior to me in those noble sentiments which animate my soul. . . . If my condition cannot be ameliorated, remove me from Brienne; put me to some mechanical trade, if it must be so; let me but find myself among my equals and I will answer for it, I will soon be their superior. You may judge of my despair by my proposal; once more I repeat it; I would sooner be foreman in a workshop than be sneered at in a first-rate academy."

In the academy Napoleon remained, however, censured by his parents for his ambitious, haughty spirit. He was gloomy and reserved and had few companions, feeling even at this early age that he was superior to those around him. He admired Cromwell, though he thought the English general incomplete in his conquests. He read Plutarch and the *Commentaries* of Cæsar and determined that his own career should be that of a soldier, though he wrote again to the straitened household in Corsica, declaring, "He who cannot afford to make a lawyer of his son, makes him a carpenter."

He chose for the moment to disregard the family ties which were especially strong among the island community. "Let my brothers' education be less expensive," he urged, "let my sisters work to maintain themselves." There was a touch of ruthless egotism in this spirit, yet the Corsican had real love for his own kindred as he showed in later life. But at this period he panted for fame and glory so ardently that he would readily sacrifice those nearest to him. He could not bear to feel that his unusual abilities might never find full scope; he was certain that one day he would be able to repay any generosity that was shown to him.

The French Revolution broke out and Napoleon saw his first chance of distinction. He was well recommended by his college for a position in the artillery, despite the strange report of the young student's character and manners which was written for the private perusal of those making the appointment.

"Napoleon Buonaparte, a Corsican by birth, reserved and studious, neglectful of all pleasures for study; delights in important and judicious readings; extremely attentive to methodical sciences, moderately so as to others; well versed in mathematics and geography; silent, a lover of solitude, whimsical, haughty, excessively prone to egotism, speaking but little, pithy in his answers, quick and severe in repartee, possessed of much self-love, ambitious, and high in expectation."

Soon after the fall of the Bastille, Napoleon placed himself at the head of the revolutionary party in Ajaccio, hoping to become the La Fayette of a National Guard which he tried to establish on the isle of Corsica. He aspired to be the commander of a paid native guard if such could be created, and was not unreasonable in his ambition since he was the only Corsican officer trained at a royal military school. But France rejected the proposal for such a force to be established, and Napoleon had to act on his own initiative. He forfeited his French commission by outstaying his furlough in 1792. Declared a deserter, he saw slight chance of promotion to military glory. Indeed he would probably have been tried by court-martial and shot, had not Paris been in confusion owing to the outbreak of the French war against European allies. He decided to lead the rebels of Corsica, and tried to get possession of Ajaccio at the Easter Festival.

This second attempt to raise an insurrection ended in the entire Buonaparte family being driven by the wrathful Corsicans to France, which henceforth was their adopted country. The Revolution blazed forth and King and Queen went to the scaffold, while treason that might, in time of peace, have served to send an officer to death, proved a stepping-stone to high rank and promotion. It was a civil war, and in it Napoleon was first to show his extraordinary skill in military tactics. He had command of the artillery besieging Toulon in 1793 and was marked as a man of merit, receiving the command of a brigade and passing as a general of artillery into the foreign war which Republican France waged against all Europe.

The command of the army of Italy was offered Napoleon by Barras, who was one of the new Directory formed to rule the Republic. A rich wife seemed essential for a poor young man with boundless ambitions just unfolding. Barras had taken up the Corsican, and arranged an introduction for him to Josephine Beauharnais, the beautiful widow of a noble who had been a victim of the Reign of Terror. He had previously made the acquaintance of Josephine's young son Eugene, when the boy came to ask that his father's sword might be restored to him.

Josephine pleased the suitor by her amiability, and was attracted in turn by his ardent nature. She was in a position to advance his interests through her intimacy with Barras, who promised that Napoleon should hold a great position in the army if she became his wife. She married Napoleon in March 1796, undaunted by the prediction: "You will be a queen and yet you will not sit on a throne." Napoleon's career may then be said to have begun in earnest. It was the dawn of a new age in Europe, where France stood forth as a predominant power. Austria was against her as the avenger of Marie Antoinette, France's ill-fated Queen, who had been Maria Theresa's daughter. England and Russia were in alliance, though Russia was an uncertain and disloyal ally.

Want of money might have daunted one less eager for success than the young Napoleon. He was, however, planning a campaign in Italy as an indirect means of attacking Austria. He addressed his soldiers boldly, promising to lead them into the most fruitful plains in the world. " Rich provinces, great cities will be in your power," he assured them. "There you will find honour, fame, and wealth." His first success was notable, but it did not satisfy the inordinate craving of his nature. " In our days," he told Marmont, " no one has conceived anything great; it falls to me to give the example."

From the outset he looked upon himself as a general independent of the Republic. He was rich in booty, and could pay his men without appealing to the well-nigh exhausted public funds. Silently, he pursued his own policy in war, and that was very different from the policy of any general who had gone before him. He treated with the Pope as a great prince might have treated, offering protection to persecuted priests who were marked out by the Directory as their enemies. He seized property everywhere, scorning to observe neutrality. Forgetting his Italian blood, he carried off many pictures and statues from the Italian galleries that they might be sent to France. He showed now his audacity and the amazing energy of his plans of conquest. The effect of the horror and disorders of Revolutionary wars had been to deprive him of all scruples. He despised a Republic, and despised the French nation as unfit for Republicanism. " A republic of thirty millions of people ! " he exclaimed as he conquered Italy, " with our morals, our vices ! How is such a thing possible ? The nation wants a chief, a chief covered with glory, not theories of government, phrases, idealogical essays, that the French do not understand. They want some playthings; that will be enough; they will play with them and let themselves be led, always supposing they are cleverly prevented from seeing the goal toward which they are moving." But the wily Corsican did not often speak so plainly! Aiming at imperial power, he was careful to dissimulate his intentions since the army supporting him was Republican in sympathy.

Napoleon had achieved the conquest of Italy when only twenty-seven. In 1796 he entered Milan amid the acclamations of the people, his troops passing beneath a triumphal arch. The Italians from that day adopted his tricolour ensign.

The Directory gave the conqueror the command of the army which was to be used against England. The old desperate rivalry had broken out again now that the French saw a chance of regaining power in India. It was Napoleon's purpose to wage war in Egypt, and he needed much money for his campaign in a distant country. During the conquest of Italy he had managed to secure money from the Papal chests and he could rely, too, on the vast spoil taken from Berne when the old constitution of the Swiss was overthrown and a new Republic founded. He took Malta, "the strongest place in Europe," and proceeded to occupy Alexandria in 1798. In the following February he marched on Cairo.

England's supremacy at sea destroyed the complete success of the plans which Napoleon was forming. He had never thought seriously of the English admiral Nelson till his own fleet was shattered by him in a naval engagement at Aboukir. After that, he understood that he had to reckon with a powerful enemy.

The Man from Corsica

The Turks had decided to anticipate Napoleon's plan for securing Greece her freedom by preparing a vast army in Syria. The French took the town of Jaffa by assault, but had to retire from the siege of Acre. The expedition was not therefore a success, though Napoleon won a victory over the Turkish army at Aboukir. The English triumphed in Egypt and were fortunate enough to win back Malta, which excluded France from the Mediterranean. Napoleon eluded with difficulty the English cruisers and returned to France, where he rapidly rose to power, receiving, after a kind of revolution, the title of First Consul. He was to hold office for ten years and receive a salary of half a million francs. In reality, a strong monarchy had been created. The people of France, however, still fancied themselves a free Republic.

War was declared on France by Austria and England in 1800, and the First Consul saw himself raised to the pinnacle of military glory. He defeated the Austrians at Marengo, while his only rival, Moreau, won the great battle of Hohenlinden. At Marengo, the general whom Napoleon praised above all others fell dead on the field of battle. The conqueror himself mourned Desaix most bitterly, since " he loved glory for glory's sake and France above everything." But "Alas! it is not permitted to weep," Napoleon said, overcoming the weakness as he judged it. He had done now with wars waged on a small scale, and would give Europe a time of peace before venturing on vaster enterprises. The victory of Marengo on June 14th, 1800, wrested Italy again from Austria, who had regained possession and power in the peninsula. It also saved France from invasion. Austria was obliged to accept an armistice, a humiliation she had not foreseen when she arrayed her mighty armies against the First Consul. Napoleon gloried in this success, proposing to Rouget de Lisle, the writer of the *Marseillaise*, that a battle-hymn should commemorate the coming of peace with victory.

The Treaty of Lunéville, 1801, settled Continental strife so effectually that Napoleon was free to attend to the internal affairs of the French Republic. The Catholic Church was restored by the *Concordat*, but made to depend on the new ruler instead of the Bourbon party. The Treaty of Amiens in 1802 provided for a truce to the hostilities of France and England.

With the world at peace, the Consulate had leisure to reconstruct the constitution. The capability of Napoleon ensured the successful performance of this mighty task. He was bent on giving a firm government to France since this would help him to reach the height of his ambitions. He drew up the famous Civil Code on which the future laws were based, and restored the ancient University of France. Financial reforms led to the establishment of the Bank of France, and Napoleon's belief that merit should be recognized publicly to the enrolment of distinguished men in a Legion of Honour.

The remarkable vigour and intelligence of this military leader was displayed in the reforms he made where all had been confusion. France was weary of the republican government which had brought her to the verge of bankruptcy and ruin, and inclined to look favourably on the idea of a monarchy.

Napoleon determined that this should be the monarchy of a Buonaparte, not that of a Bourbon. The Church had ceased to support the claims of Louis XVI's brother. Napoleon had won the *noblesse*, too, by his feats of arms, and the peacemaker's decrees had reconciled the foreign cabinets. It ended, as the prudent had foreseen, in the First Consul choosing for himself the old military title of Emperor.

His coronation on December 2nd, 1804, was a ceremony of magnificence, unequalled since the fall of the majestic Bourbons. Napoleon placed the sacred diadem on his own head and then on the head of Josephine, who knelt to receive it. His aspect was gloomy as he received this symbol of successful ambition, for the mass of the people was silent and he was uneasy at the usurpation of a privilege which was not his birthright. The authority of the Pope had confirmed his audacious action, but he was afraid of the attitude of his army. "The greatest man in the world" Kléber had proclaimed him, after the crushing of the Turks at Aboukir in Egypt. There was work to do before he reached the summit whence he might justly claim such admiration. He found court life at St Cloud very wearisome after the peace of his residence at Malmaison.

"I have not a moment to myself. I ought to have been the wife of a humble cottager," Josephine wrote in a fit of impatience at the restraints imposed upon an Empress. But she clung to the title desperately when she knew that it would be taken from her. She had been Napoleon's wife for fourteen years, but no heir had been born to inherit the power and to continue the dynasty which he hoped to found. She was divorced in 1809, when he married Marie Louise of Austria.

Peace could not last with Napoleon upon the throne of France, determined as he was in his resolution to break the supremacy of the foe across the Channel.

He had not forgotten Egypt and his failure in the Mediterranean. He resolved to crush the English fleet by a union of the fleets of Europe. He was busied with daring projects to invade England from Boulogne. The distance by sea was so short that panic seized the island-folk, who had listened to wild stories about the "Corsican ogre." Nelson was the hope of the nation in the year of danger, 1805, when the English fleet gained the glorious victory of Trafalgar and saved England from the dreaded invasion. But the hero of Trafalgar met his death in the hour of success, and, before the year closed, Napoleon's victory at Austerlitz destroyed the coalition led by the Austrian Emperor and the Tsar and caused a whole continent to tremble before the conqueror. The news of this battle, indeed, hastened the death of Pitt, the English minister, who had struggled nobly against the aggrandisement of France. He knew that the French Empire would rise to the height of fame, and that the coalition of Russia, Prussia, and Austria would fall disastrously.

"The Prussians wish to receive a lesson," Napoleon declared, flushed by the magnificence of his late efforts. He defeated them at Jena and Auerstädt, and entered Berlin to take the sword and sash of Frederick the Great as well as the Prussian standards. He did honour to that illustrious Emperor by forbidding the passage of the colours and eagles over the place where Frederick reposed, and he declared himself satisfied with Frederick's personal belongings as conferring more honour than any other treasures.

By the Treaty of Tilsit, concluded with Alexander of Russia on a raft upon the River Niemen, Prussia suffered new humiliations. The proud creation of Frederick's military genius had vanished. There was

The Man from Corsica

even undue haste to give up fortresses to the conqueror. The country was partitioned between Russia, Saxony, and Westphalia, created for the rule of Jerome Buonaparte, Napoleon's younger brother. He set up kings now with the ease of a born autocrat. His brother Joseph became King of Naples, and his brother Louis King of Holland.

A new nobility sprang up, for honours must be equally showered on the great generals who had helped to win his victories. The new Emperor was profuse in favour, not believing in disinterested affection. He paid handsomely for the exercise of the humours, known as his "vivacités," entering in a private book such items as "Fifteen napoleons to Menneval for a box on the ear, a war-horse to my aide-de-camp Mouton for a kick, fifteen hundred *arpens* in the imperial forests to Bassano for having dragged him round my room by the hair."

These rewards drained the empire and provided a grievance against the Corsican adventurer who had dared to place all Europe under the rule of Buonaparte. The family did not bear their elevation humbly, but demanded ever higher rank and office. Joseph was raised to the exalted state of King of Spain after the lawful king had been expelled by violence. The patriotism of the Spanish awoke and found an echo in the neighbouring kingdom of Portugal. Napoleon was obliged to send his best armies to the Peninsula where the English hero, Sir Arthur Wellesley, was pushing his way steadily toward the Pyrenees and the French frontier.

The expedition to Russia had been partly provoked by the Emperor's marriage with Marie Louise of Austria. There had been talk of a marriage between Napoleon and the Tsar's sister. Then the arrangement of Tilsit had become no longer necessary after the humbling of Austria. Napoleon wished to throw off his ally, Alexander, and was ready to use as a pretext for war Russia's refusal to adopt his " continental system " fully. This system, designed to crush the commercial supremacy of England by forbidding other countries to trade with her, was thus, as events were to prove, the cause of Napoleon's own downfall.

The enormous French army made its way to Russia and entered Moscow, the ancient capital, which the inhabitants burned and deserted. In the army's retreat from the city in the depth of winter, thousands died of cold and hunger, and 30,000 men had already fallen in the fruitless victory at Borodino.

Napoleon was nearing his downfall as he struggled across the continent in the dreadful march which reduced an army of a quarter of a million men to not more than twelve thousand. He had to meet another failure and the results of a destructive imperial policy in 1814, when he was defeated at Leipzig by Austria, Russia, and Prussia, who combined most desperately against him. The Allies issued at Frankfort their famous manifesto " Peace with France but war against the Empire." They compelled Napoleon to abdicate, and restored the Bourbon line. A court was formed for Louis XVIII at the Tuileries, while Napoleon was sent to Elba.

Louis XVI's brother, the Count of Artois, came back, still admired by the faded beauties of the Restoration. The pathetic figure of Louis XVI's daughter, the Duchess of Angoulême, was seen amid the forced gaieties of the new régime, and Madame de Staël haunted the court of Louis XVIII, forgetting her late revolutionary sentiments.

The Man from Corsica

Napoleon grew very weary of his inaction on the isle of Elba. He had spent all his life in military pursuits and missed the companionship of soldiers. He thought with regret of his old veterans when he welcomed the guards sent to him. Perhaps he hoped for the arrival of his wife, too, as he paced up and down the narrow walk by the sea where he took exercise daily. But Marie Louise returned to her own country.

Napoleon found some scope for his activity in the government of the island, and gave audiences regularly to the people. He might seem to have lost ambition as he read in his library or played with a tame monkey of which he made a pet, but a scheme of great audacity was forming in his mind. He resolved to go back to France once more and appeal to the armies to restore him.

The Bourbons had never become popular again with the nation which was inspired with the lust for military successes. The life in the Tuileries seemed empty and frivolous, wanting in great figures. There was little resistance when the news came that Napoleon had landed and put himself at the head of the troops at Grenoble.

He had appealed to the ancient spirit of the South which had risen before in the cause of liberty. Feudalism and the oppression of the peasants would return under the rule of the Bourbons, he assured them. They began to look upon the abdicated Emperor as the Angel of Deliverance. The people of Lyons were equally enthusiastic, winning warmer words than generally fell from the lips of Napoleon. "I love you," he cried, and bore them with him to the capital. He entered the Tuileries at night, and again the eagle of the Empire flew from steeple to steeple on every church of Paris.

The Hundred Days elapsed between the liberation from the Bourbons and Napoleon's last struggle for supremacy. The King made a feeble effort against the Emperor. It was, however, the united armies of England and Prussia that met the French on the field of Waterloo in 1815. From March 13th to June 22nd Napoleon had had time to realize the might of Wellesley, now Duke of Wellington. The splendid powers of the once indefatigable French general were declining. Napoleon, who had not been wont to take advice, now asked the opinions of others. The dictator, so rapid in coming to a decision, hesitated in the hour of peril. He was defeated at Waterloo on June 18th, 1815, by Blücher and Wellington together. The battle raged from the middle of morning to eight o'clock in the evening and ended in the rout of the French troops. The Emperor performed a second time the ceremony of abdication, and, his terrible will being broken, surrendered on board the *Bellerophon* to the English.

The English Government feared a second return like the triumphant flight from Elba. No enemy had ever been so terrible to England as Napoleon. He must be removed altogether from the continent of Europe. St Helena was chosen as the place of imprisonment, and Sir Hudson Lowe put over him as, in some sort, a gaoler. A certain amount of personal freedom was accorded, but the captive on the lonely rock did not live to regain liberty. He died in 1821 on a day of stormy weather, uttering *tête d'armée* in the last moments of delirium.

Chapter XVI

"God and the People"

THE diplomatists who assembled at the Congress of Vienna to settle the affairs of Europe, so strangely disturbed by the vehement career of that soldier-genius, Napoleon, had it in their minds to restore as far as possible the older forms of government.

Italy was restless, unwilling to give up the patriotic dreams inspired by the conqueror. The people saw with dismay that the hope of unity was over since the peninsula, divided into four states, was parcelled out again and placed under the hated yoke of Austria. Soldiers from Piedmont and Lombardy, from Venice and Naples, Parma and Modena, had fought side by side, sharing the glory of a military despot and willing to endure a tyranny that gave them a firm administration and a share of justice. They saw that prosperity for their land would follow the more regular taxation and the abolition of the social privileges oppressive to the peasants. They looked forward to increase of trade as roads were made and bridges built, and they welcomed the chance of education and the preparation for a national life. Napoleon had always held before them the picture of a great Italian State, freed from foreign princes and realizing the promise of the famous Middle Ages.

Yet Napoleon had done nothing to forward the cause of Italian freedom before his final exile. The Italians would have made Eugene Beauharnais king of a united Italy, but Eugene was loyal to the stepfather who had placed under his power the territory lying between the Alps and the centre of the peninsula. Murat, Napoleon's brother-in-law, would have grasped the sceptre, for he was devoured by overwhelming ambition. He owed his rapid advance from obscurity to the position of a general to the Corsican, whose own career had led him to help men to rise by force of merit. Murat bore a part in the struggle for Italy when the cry was ever Liberty. A new spirit had come upon the indolent inheritors of an ancient name. They were burning to achieve the freedom of Italy, and hearkened only to the voice that offered independence.

Prince Metternich, the absolute ruler of Austria, set aside the conflicting claims, and parcelled out the states among petty rulers all looking to him for political guidance. Italy was "only a geographical expression," he remarked with satisfaction. Cadets of the Austrian house held Tuscany and Modena, and Marie Louise, the ex-empress, was installed at Parma. Pius VII took up the papal domain in Central Italy with firmer grasp. Francis II, Emperor of Austria, seized Venice and Lombardy, while a Bourbon, in the person of Ferdinand I, received Naples and Sicily, a much disputed heritage. Victor Emmanuel, King of Sardinia, received also the Duchies of Savoy and Piedmont. San Marino was a republic still, standing solitary and mournful upon the waters of the Adriatic. Italy was divided state from state, as in the medieval times, but now, alas! each state could not boast free government.

"God and the People"

Italians, eating the bread of slaves, felt that they were in bondage to Vienna. Metternich had determined they should know no master but himself, and all attempts to rebel were closely watched by spies. The police force allowed nothing to be printed or spoken against the government that was strong to condemn disorder. There were ardent souls longing to fight for the cause of Italy and Liberty. There were secret societies resolving desperate measures. There was discontent everywhere to war with Metternich's distrust of social progress.

The sufferings of rebel leaders moved the compassion of Giuseppe Mazzini, the son of a clever physician in the town of Genoa. He was only a boy when he was accosted by a refugee, whose wild countenance told a story of cruelty and oppression. From that moment, he realized the degradation of Italy and chose the colour of mourning for his clothes; he began to study the heroic struggles which had made martyrs of his countrymen in late years, and he began to form visionary projects which led him from the study of literature—his first sacrifice. He had aspired to a literary career, and renounced it to throw himself into the duties he owed to countrymen and country.

In 1827, Mazzini joined the Carbonari, or Charcoalmen, a society which worked in different countries with one aim—opposition to the despot and the legitimist. The young man of twenty-two was impressed, no doubt, by the solemn oath of initiation which he had to take over a bared dagger, but he soon had to acknowledge that the efforts of the Carbonari were doomed to dismal failure. Membership was confined too much to the professional class, and there were too few appeals to the youth of Italy. Treachery was rife among the different sections of the wide-spreading organization. It was easy for a man to be condemned on vague suspicions. When Mazzini was arrested, he had to be acquitted of the charge of conspiracy because it was impossible to find two witnesses, but general disapproval was expressed of his mode of life. The governor of Genoa spoke very harshly of the student's habit of walking about at night in thoughtful silence. "What on earth has he, at his age, to think about?" he demanded angrily. "We don't like young people thinking without our knowing the subjects of their thoughts."

The "glorious days of July," 1830, freed the French from a monarchy which threatened liberal principles, and roused the discontented in other countries to make fresh efforts for freedom. Certain ordinances, published on July 25th by the French Ministry, suspended the freedom of the press, altered the law of election to the Chambers of Deputies, and suppressed a number of Liberal journals. Paris rose to resist, and on July 28th, men of the Faubourg St Antoine took possession of the Hôtel de Ville, hoisting the tricolour flag again. Charles X was deposed in favour of Louis Philippe, the Citizen-King, who was a son of that Duke of Orleans once known as Philippe Equality. "A popular throne with republican institutions" thus replaced the absolute monarchy of the Bourbons. There was an eager belief in other lands that the new King of France would support attempts to abolish tyranny, but Louis Philippe was afraid of losing power, and in Italy an insurrection in favour of the new freedom was overawed by an army sent from Austria. The time was not yet come for the blow to be struck which would fulfil the object of the

Carbonari by driving every Austrian from their country.

Mazzini passed into exile, realizing that there had been some fatal defect in the organization of a society whose attempts met with such failure. He was confirmed in his belief that the youth of Italy must be roused and educated to win their own emancipation. "Youth lives on freedom," he said, "grows great in enthusiasm and faith." Then he made his appeal for the enrolment of these untried heroes. "Consecrate them with a lofty mission; influence them with emulation and praise; spread through their ranks the word of fire, the word of inspiration; speak to them of country, of glory, of power, of great memories." So he recalled the past to them, and the genius which had dazzled the world as it rose from the land of strange passion and strange beauty. Dante was more than a poet to him. He had felt the same love of unity, had looked to the future and seen the day when the bond-slave should shake off the yoke and declare a national unity.

The young Italians rallied round the standard of the patriot, whose words lit in them the spark of sacrifice. They received his adjurations gladly, promising to obey them. He pointed out a thorny road, but the reward was at the end, the illumination of the soul which crowns each great endeavour. Self had to be forgotten and family ties broken if they held back from the claims of country. Mazzini thought the family sacred, but he bade parents give up their sons in time of national danger. It was the duty of every father to fit his children to be citizens. Humanity made demands which some could only satisfy by submitting to long martyrdom.

served Napoleon. He was in exile at Geneva, and chose Savoy as the base of operations. The whole attempt failed miserably, and hardly a shot was fired.

Even the refuge in Switzerland was lost after this rising. He fled from house to house, hunted and despairing with the curses of former allies in his ears now that he had brought distress upon them. He could not even get books as a solace for his weary mind, and clothes and money were difficult to obtain since his friends knew how importunate was Young Italy in demands, and how easily he yielded to the beggar. Bitterness came to him, threatening to mar his fine nature and depriving him of courage. Italy had sunk into apathy again, and he knew not how to rouse her. He bowed his head and asked pardon of God because he had dared to sacrifice in that last effort the lives of many others.

Mazzini rose again, resolved to do without friends and kindred, if duty should forbid those consolations. He thought of the lives of Juvenal, urging the Roman to ask for " the soul that has no fear of death and that endures life's pain and labour calmly." He gave up dreams of love and ambition for himself, feeling that the only way for Italy to succeed was to place religion before politics. The eighteenth century had rebelled for rights and selfish interests, and the nineteenth century was preparing to follow the same teaching. Rights would not help to create the ideal government of Mazzini. Men fought for the right to worship, and sometimes cared not to use the privilege when they had obtained it. Men demanded votes and sold them, after making an heroic struggle.

In 1837, London received the exiles who could find no welcome elsewhere. The fog and squalor of the city offered a dreary prospect to patriots from a land of sun and colour. Poverty cut them off from companionship with their equals. Mazzini was content to live on rice and potatoes, but the brothers Ruffini had moments of reaction. The joint household suffered from an invasion of needy exiles. There were quarrels and visits to the pawnshops. Debt and the difficulty of earning money added a sordid element.

Mazzini made some friends when the Ruffinis left England. He knew Carlyle, the great historian, and visited his house frequently. The two men differed on many points, but "served the same god" in essentials. Carlyle had an admiration for the despot, while the Italian loathed tyranny. There was hot debate in the drawing-room where the exile talked of freedom, blissfully unconscious that his wet boots were spoiling his host's carpet! There were sublime discussions of the seer Dante, after which Carlyle would dismiss his guest in haste because he longed to return to his own study.

The prophet had lost his vision but it came back to him, working among the wretched little peasants, brought from Italy to be exploited by the organ-grinders. He taught the boys himself and found friends to tend them. Grisi, the famed singer, would help to earn money for the school in Hatton Garden.

To reach the working classes had become the great aspiration of Mazzini. "Italy of the People" was the phrase he loved henceforward. He roused popular sympathy by a new paper which he edited, the *Apostolato Popolare*. It served a definite end in rousing the spirit that was abroad, clamouring for nationalism.

Revolution broke out in 1847 when Sicily threw off the Bourbon yoke, and Naples obtained a constitution in the streets where he would have kept the flag flying which had been lowered by the Assembly. He was grey with the fierce endurance of the two months' siege, but his heart bade him not desert his post from any fear of death. Secretly he longed for the assassin's knife, for then he would have shed the blood of sacrifice for the cause of patriotism.

Chapter XVII

"For Italy and Victor Emmanuel!"

THE year of Revolution, beginning with most glorious hopes, ended disastrously for the Italian patriots. Princes had allied with peasants in eager furtherance of the cause of freedom but defeat took away their faith. The soldiers lost belief in the leaders of the movement and belief, alas! in the ideals for which they had been fighting.

Charles Albert, the King of Sardinia, continued to struggle on alone when adversities had deprived his most faithful partisans of their zeal for fighting. He had once been uncertain and vacillating in mind, but he became staunch in his later days and able to reply courageously to the charges which his enemies brought against him. He mustered some 80,000 men and put them under Polish leaders—a grave mistake, since the soldiers were prejudiced by the strange foreign aspect of their officers and began the war without enthusiasm for their generals.

Field-Marshal Radetsky, a redoubtable enemy, only brought the same numbers to the field, but he had the advantage of being known as a conquering hero. His cry was "To Turin!" but the bold Piedmontese rallied to defend their town and spread the news of joyful victory throughout the Italian peninsula. Other their ancient enemy of Austria. Cold and hunger would be theirs, and the weariness of constant marches. Death would be the lot of many in their ranks, the cruel tortures of their gaolers. All men were outlaws who had defended Rome, the Republic, to the last, and bread and water might be refused to them within the confines of their country.

The cry for war sounded, and Garibaldi led three thousand men, including Ugo Bassi and the noblest of knight-errants. The attempt to reach Venice was frustrated by a storm, and Anita died miserably in a peasant's cottage, where she was dragged for shelter. Garibaldi fled to the United States, and never saw again many of his bold companions. Venice was left of dire necessity to defend herself from Austria. She had sworn to resist to the last, and President Manin refused to surrender even when cholera came upon the town and the citizens were famished. He appealed to England, but only got advice to make terms with the besiegers. He capitulated in the end because the town was bombarded by the Austrian army, and he feared that the conquerors would exercise a fell vengeance if the city still resisted. There was nothing left to eat after the eighteen months' siege of Venice. Manin left for Marseilles, mourned bitterly by the Venetians. His very door-step was broken by the Austrians, who found his name upon it. Ugo Bassi had kissed it, voicing the sentiment of many. "Next to God and Italy—before the Pope—Manin!"

Victor Emmanuel, the young King of Sardinia, had won no such popularity, suffering from the prejudice against his family, the House of Savoy, and against his wife, an Austrian by birth. He came to the throne at a dark time, succeeding to a royal inheritance of ruin and misery. The army had been disgraced, and the exchequer was empty. He had the dignity of a king and remarkable boldness, but it would have been hard for him to have guided Italy without his adviser and friend, the Count Cavour.

Mazzini, the prophet, and Garibaldi, the soldier, had won the hearts of Italians devoted to the cause of Italy. Cavour suffered the same distrust as Victor Emmanuel, but he knew his task and performed it. He was the statesman who made the government and created the present stable monarchy. He had to be satisfied with less than the Republican enthusiasts. He had few illusions, and believed that in politics it was possible to choose the end but rarely possible to choose the means.

Born in Piedmont in 1810, the statesman was of noble birth and sufficient wealth, being a godson of Pauline, sister of the great Napoleon. He joined the army as an engineer in 1828, but found the life little to his taste since he was not allowed to express his opinions freely. He resigned in 1831 and retired to the country, where he was successful as a farmer. He travelled extensively for those days, and visited England, where he studied social problems.

Of all foreigners, Cavour, perhaps, benefited most largely by a study of the English Parliament from the outside. He was present at debates, and wrote articles on Free Trade and the English Poor Law. He had enlightened views, and wished to promote the interests of Italy by raising her to the position of a power in Europe. He set to work to bring order into the finances of Sardinia, but the King recognized his minister's unpopularity by the nickname *bestia neira*. He had a seat in 1848 in the first Parliament of Piedmont, and was Minister of Commerce and Agriculture later. He pushed on reforms to benefit the trade and industries of Italy without troubling to consult the democrats, his enemies. His policy was liberal, but he intended to go slowly. "Piedmont must begin by raising herself, by re-establishing in Europe as well as in Italy, a position and a credit equal to her ambition. Hence there must be a policy unswerving in its aims but flexible and various as to the means employed." Cavour's character was summed up in these words. He distrusted violent measures, and yet could act with seeming rashness in a crisis when prudence would mean failure.

Prime Minister in 1852, he saw an opportunity two years later of winning fame for Piedmont. The Russians were resisting the western powers which defended the dominions of the Porte. Ministers resigned and the country marvelled, but Cavour signed a pledge to send forces of 15,000 men to the Crimea to help Turkey against Russia. It would be well to prove that Italy retained the military virtues of her history after the defeat of Novara, he said in reply to all expostulations. The result showed the statesman's wisdom and justified his daring. The Sardinians distinguished themselves in the Crimea, and Italy was able to enter into negotiations with the great European powers who arranged the Peace of Paris.

The Congress of Paris was the time for Cavour to gain sympathy for the woes of Italian states, still subject to the tyrannous sway of Austria. He denounced the enslavement of Naples also, and brought odium upon King Ferdinand, but "Austria," he said, "is the arch-enemy of Italian independence; the permament danger to the only free nation in Italy, the nation I have the honour to represent."

England confined herself to expressions of sympathy, but Louis Napoleon, now Emperor of France, seemed likely to become an ally. He met Cavour at Plombières, a watering place in the Vosges, in July 1858, and entered into a formal compact to expel the Austrians from Italy. The final arrangements were made in the following spring in Paris. "It is done," said Cavour, the minister triumphant. "We have made some history, and now to dinner."

Mazzini, in England, read of the alliance with gloomy misgivings, for, as a Republican, he distrusted the President of France who had made himself an Emperor. He said that Napoleon III would work now for his own ends. He protested in vain. Garibaldi rejoiced and returned from Caprera, where he had been trying to plant a garden on a barren island.

Cavour fought against some prejudice when he offered to enrol Garibaldi and his followers in the army of Sardinia. Charles Albert had refused the hero's sword in the days of his bitter struggle, and the regular officers still looked askance on the Revolutionary captain.

But the Austrian troops were countless, numbering recruits from the Tyrol and Bohemia, from the valleys of Styria and the Hungarian steppes. There was need of a vast army to oppose them. The French soldiers fought gallantly, yet they were inferior to the Austrians in discipline. When the allies had won the hard contested fight of Montebello it was good to think of that band of 3000, singing as they marched, "*Addio mia bella, addio,*" like the knights of legend. They crossed Lake Maggiore into the enemy's own country, and took all the district of the Lowland Lakes.

In June, the allies won the victory of Magenta, and on the 8th of that month, King and Emperor entered Milan flushed with victory. The Austrians had fled, and the keys of the city were in the possession of Victor Emmanuel.

The Emperor of Austria, Francis Joseph, had assumed command of the army when the great battle of Solferino was fought amidst the wondrous beauty of Italian scenery in an Italian summer. It was June 24th, and the peasant reaped the harvest of Lombardy, wondering if he should reap for the conqueror the next day. The French officers won great glory as they charged up the hills, which must be taken before they could succeed in storming Solferino. After a fierce struggle of six hours, the streets of the little town were filled with the bodies of the dead and dying. By the evening, the victory of the allies over Austria was certain.

Napoleon III had kept his promise to the Italian people, who were encouraged by a success of the Piedmontese army under Victor Emmanuel at San Martino. But he disappointed them cruelly by stopping short in his victorious career and sending General Fleury to the Austrian camp to demand an armistice. Europe was amazed when the preliminaries of peace were signed, for it was generally expected that Austria would be brought to submission. Italy was in despair, for Venetia had not yet been won for them.

Cavour raged with fury, regretting that he had trusted Napoleon and trusted his King, Victor Emmanuel, who agreed to the proposals for an armistice. Now he heaped them with reproaches because they had given up the Italian cause. He resigned office in bitterness for it was he who had concluded the alliance of France and Italy.

Napoleon returned to France, pursued by the indignation of the country he had come to deliver. He complained of their ingratitude, though he might have known that Lombardy would not accept freedom at the cost of Venice. He was execrated when the price of his assistance was demanded. France claimed Nice and Savoy as French provinces henceforth. Savoy was the country of Victor Emmanuel, and Nice the honoured birthplace of the idolized Garibaldi!

Garibaldi was chosen by the people of Nice for the new Chamber of 1860, for they hoped that he would make an effort to save his native town. He had some idea of raising a revolution against French rule, but decided to free Sicily as a mightier enterprise. Victor Emmanuel completed the sacrifice which gave "the cradle of his race" to the foreigner. He was reconciled to the cession at length because he believed that Italy had gained much already.

Cavour did not openly approve of the attack which Garibaldi was preparing to make upon the Bourbon's sovereignty. Many said that he did his best to frustrate the plans of the soldier because there was hostility between them. Garibaldi could not forgive the cession of Nice to which the statesmen had, ere this, assented. He was bitter in his feeling toward Victor Emmanuel's minister, but he was loyal to Victor Emmanuel. His band of volunteers, known as the Thousand, marched in the King's name, and the chief refused to enrol those whose Republican sentiments made them dislike the idea of Italian unity. "Italy and Victor Emmanuel," the cry of the Hunters of the Alps, was the avowed object of his enterprise.

Garibaldi sailed amid intense excitement, proudly promising " a new and glorious jewel " to the King of Sardinia, if the venture were successful. The standard of revolt had already been raised by Rosalino Pilo, the handsome Sicilian noble, whose whole life had been devoted to the cause of country. The insurgents awaited Garibaldi with a feverish desire for success against the Neapolitan army, which numbered 150,000 men. They knew that the leader brought only few soldiers but that they were picked men. Strange stories had been told of Garibaldi's success in warfare, being due to supernatural intervention. The prayers of his beautiful old peasant-mother were said to have prevailed till her death, when her spirit came to hold converse with the hero before battle.

The Red-shirts landed at Marsala, a thousand strong, packed into merchant vessels by a patriotic owner. Garibaldi led them to the mountain city of Salemi, which had opposed the Bourbon dynasty warmly. There he proclaimed himself dictator of Sicily in the name of Victor Emmanuel, soon to be ruler of all Italy. Peasants joined the Thousand, armed with rusty pistols and clad in picturesque goat-skins. They were received with honour by the chief, who was pleased to see that Sicily was bent on freedom. A Franciscan friar threw himself upon his knees before the mighty leader and asked to join the expedition. " Come with us, you will be our Ugo Bassi," Garibaldi said, remembering with a pang the defence of Rome and the fate of the defenders.

At Palermo, the capital of Sicily, the Neapolitan soldiers were awaiting the arrival of the Thousand. They ventured to attack first, being very strong in

The Meeting of Victor Emmanuel and Garibaldi
Pietro Aldi

numbers. The bravest might have feared to oppose the royal troops with such a disadvantage, but Garibaldi held firm when there were murmurs of surrender. "Here we *die*," he said, and the great miracle was accomplished. "Yesterday we fought and conquered," the chief wrote to the almost despairing Pilo. The two forces joined and Pilo fell, struck by a bullet. It was May 27th when Garibaldi entered the gates of Palermo.

The bells were hammered by the inhabitants, delighted to welcome the brave Thousand to their city. There was still a fierce struggle within the walls, and the Neapolitan fleet bombarded the town. An armistice was granted on May 30th, for the Royalists needed food and did not realize that Garibaldi's ammunition was exhausted. He refused to submit to any humiliating terms that might be offered to Palermo. He threatened to renew hostilities if the enemy still thought of them. All declared for war, though they knew how such a war must have ended. It was by the Royalists' act that the evacuation of the city was concluded.

The Revolution had succeeded elsewhere, and for the last time the Bourbon flag was hoisted in Sicilian waters. The conquest of Sicily had occupied but a few days. The Dictator proceeded thence to the south of Italy and advanced on the Neapolitan kingdom.

Victor Emmanuel would have checked the hero of Palermo, and Cavour was thoroughly uneasy. No official consent had been given for this daring act of aggression, and foreign powers wrote letters of protest, while King Francis II, the successor of Ferdinand, held out such bribes as fifty million francs and the Neapolitan navy to aid in liberating Venice. France induced the King of Sardinia to make an effort to restrain the popular soldier. Garibaldi promised Victor Emmanuel to obey him when he had made him King of Italy.

At Volturno the decisive battle was fought on the first day of October 1860, the birthday of King Francis. "Victory all along the line" was the message sent by Garibaldi to Naples after ten hours' fighting. There had been grave fears expressed by Cavour that the army would march on Rome and expel the French after this conclusion. But the King was advancing toward the south of Italy to prevent any move which would provoke France, and Garibaldi, marching north, dismounted from his horse when he met the Piedmontese, and walking up to Victor Emmanuel, hailed him King of Italy. Naples and Sicily, with Umbria and the Marches, decided in favour of a united sceptre under the House of Savoy. It was Garibaldi's proclamation to the people which urged them to receive the new King with peace and affection. "No more political colours, no more parties, no more discords," he hoped there would be from the 7th of November, 1860. It was on that day that the king-maker and the King together entered Naples. Garibaldi refused all the honours which his sword had won, and left for his island-home at Caprera, a poor man still, but one whose name could stir all Europe.

The Italian kingdom was proclaimed by the new Parliament which met in February 1861, at Turin. All parts of Italy were represented save Rome and Venice, and King Victor Emmanuel II entered on his reign as ruler of Italy "by the Grace of God and the will of the nation."

Chapter XVIII
The Third Napoleon

ITALY was free, but Italy was not yet united as patriots such as Garibaldi had hoped that it might be. Venice and Rome must be added to the possessions of Victor Emmanuel before he could boast that he held beneath his sway all Italy between the Alps and Adriatic.

Rome, the dream of heroes, was in the power of a Pope who had to be maintained in his authority by a garrison of the French. Napoleon III clung to his alliance with the Catholic Church, and refused to withdraw his troops and leave his Papal ally defenceless, for he cared nothing about the views of Italian dreamers who longed that the Eternal City should be free.

There was romance in the life-story of this French Emperor upon whose support so many allies had come to depend. He was the son of Louis Buonaparte and Hortense Beauharnais, who was the daughter of the Empress Josephine. During the reign of Louis Philippe, this nephew of the great usurper had spent his time in dreary exile, living in London for the most part, and concealing a character of much ambition beneath a moody silent manner. He visited France in 1840 and tried to gain the throne, but was unsuccessful, for he was committed to the fortress of Ham, a state prison. He escaped in the disguise of a workman, and made a second attempt to stir the mob of Paris to revolution in the year 1848, when Europe was restless with fierce discontent. The King fled for his life, and a Republic was formed again with Louis Napoleon as President, but this did not satisfy a descendant of the great Buonaparte. He managed by the help of the army to gain the Imperial crown, never worn by the second Napoleon, who died when he was still too young to show whether he possessed the characteristics of his family. Henceforth Napoleon III of France could no longer be regarded as a mere adventurer. The Pope had come to depend on French troops for his authority, and the Italians had to pay a heavy price for French arms in their struggle against Austria.

Paris renewed its gaiety when Napoleon married his beautiful Spanish wife, Eugénie, who had royal pride though she was not of royal birth. There were hunting parties again, when the huntsmen wore brave green and scarlet instead of the Bourbon blue and silver; there were court fêtes, which made the entertainments of Louis Philippe, the honest Citizen-King, seem very dull in retrospect. The Spanish Empress longed to rival the fame of Marie Antoinette, the Austrian wife of Louis XVI who had followed that King to the scaffold. Like Marie Antoinette, she was censured for extravagances, the marriage being unpopular with all classes. The bourgeoisie or middle class refused to accept the Emperor's plea that it was better to mate with a foreigner of ordinary rank than to attempt to aggrandize the new empire by union with the daughter of some despotic king.

Yet France amused herself eagerly at the famous fêtes and hunts of Compiègne, while the third Napoleon craftily began to develop his scheme for obtaining

The Third Napoleon

influence in Europe that should make him as great a man as the Corsican whom all had dreaded. The Emperor's insignificant appearance deceived many of his compeers, who were inclined to look on him as a ruler who would be content to take a subordinate place in international affairs. He dressed in odd, startling colours, and moved awkwardly; his eyes were strangely impenetrable, and he seemed listless and indifferent, even when he was meditating some subtle plan with which to startle Europe.

Dark stories were told of the part Napoleon played in the Crimean War, when Turkey demanded help against Russia, which was crippling her army and her fleet. Many suspected that the French Emperor used England as his catspaw, and saw that the English troops bore the brunt of all the terrible disasters which befell the invaders of the south of Russia. Alma, Balaclava, and Inkerman were victories ever memorable, because the heroes of those battles had to fight against more sinister foes than the Russian troops they defeated in the field. Stores of food and clothes were delayed too long before they reached the exhausted soldiers, and there was suspicion of unjust favour shown to the French soldiers when their English allies sought a healthy camping-ground. The war ended in 1855 with the fall of Sebastopol, and it was notable afterwards that the Napoleonic splendour increased vastly, that the sham royalty seemed resolved to entertain the royal visitors who had once looked askance at him.

France began to believe that no further Revolution could disturb the Second Empire, which was secure in pride at least. Yet Austria was crushed by Prussia at the great battle of Sadowa in 1866, and the Prussian state was advancing rapidly under the government of a capable minister and king. There were few Frenchmen who had realized the importance of King Wilhelm's act when he summoned Herr Otto von Bismarck from his Pomeranian estates to be his chief political adviser. The fast increasing strength of the Prussian forces did not sufficiently impress Napoleon, who had embarked on a foolish expedition to Mexico to place an Austrian archduke on the throne, once held by the ancient Montezumas. The news of Sadowa wrung " a cry of agony " from his court of the Tuileries, where everyone had confidently expected the victory of Austria. Napoleon might have arbitrated between the two countries, but he let the golden opportunity slip by in one of those half-sullen passive moods which came upon him when he felt the depression of his bodily weakness. Prussia began to lay the foundation of German unity, excluding Austria from her territory.

Napoleon handed over Venice to Italy when it was ceded to him at the close of the Austrian war, and Garibaldi followed up this cession by an attempt on Rome, which he resolved should be the capital of Italy. He defeated the Papal troops at Monte Rotondo, which commanded Rome on the north, but he was defeated by French troops at the battle of Mentana. The repulse of the Italian hero increased the national dislike of French interference, but Napoleon only consented to evacuate Rome in 1870 when he had need of all his soldiers to carry out his boast that he would " chastise the insolence of the King of Prussia."

The Franco-Prussian War arose nominally from the quarrel about the throne of Spain, to which a prince of the Hohenzollern house had put in a claim, first obtaining permission from Wilhelm I to accept the dignity. This prince, Leopold, was not a member of the Prussian

The Third Napoleon

royal family, but he was a Prussian subject and a distant kinsman of the Kaiser. It was quite natural, therefore, that he should ask the royal sanction for his act and quite natural that Wilhelm should give it his approval if Spain made the offer of the crown.

Napoleon sought some cause of difference with Prussia, because Bismarck had refused to help him to win Belgium and Luxemburg in 1869. He was jealous of this new military power, for his own fame was far outstripped by the feats of arms accomplished by the forces of General von Moltke, the Prussian general. He thought that war against his rival might help him to regain the admiration of the French. They were humiliated by the failure of the Mexican design and saw fresh danger for their country in Italian unity and the new confederation of North Germany.

Napoleon, racked by disease, might have checked his own ambition if his Empress had not been too eager for a war. He was misled by Marshal Lebœuf into fancying that his own army was efficient enough to undertake any military campaign. He allowed his Cabinet to demand from Wilhelm I that Prince Leopold's claim to the Spanish crown, which had been withdrawn, should never be renewed by the sanction of Prussia at least. The unreasonable demand was refused, and France declared war in July 1870, eighteen years after the new empire had risen on the ruins of the Republic of the French.

The other European powers would not enter this war, though England offered to mediate between the rival powers. France and Prussia had to test the strength of their armies without allies, and neither thought how terrible the cost would be of that long national jealousy. Napoleon took the field himself, leaving Eugénie as

Regent of the French, and the King of Prussia led his own army with General Von Moltke and General Von Roon in command.

The French army invaded South Germany, but had to retreat in disorder after the battle of Wörth. The battle of Sedan on September 1st, 1870, brought the war to a conclusion, the French being routed and forced to lay down their arms. Napoleon had fought with courage, but was obliged to surrender his sword to Wilhelm I upon the battlefield. He declared that he gave up his person only, but France herself was forced to yield after the capitulation of Metz, which had resisted Prussia stoutly. The Empress had fled to England and the Emperor had been deposed. France was once more a Republic when the siege of Paris was begun.

The citizens showed strange insensibility to the danger that they ran, for they asserted that the Germans dared not invest the town. Nevertheless, Parisians drilled and armed with vigour as Prussian shells burst outside the walls and the clang of bells replaced the sounds of mirth that were habitual to Paris. Theatres were closed, to the dismay of the frivolous, whom no alarm of war would turn from their ordinary pursuits. The Opera House became a barracks, for the camps could not hold the crowds that flocked there from the provinces.

Still many ridiculed the idea of investment by the Prussian troops, and householders did not prepare for the famine that came on them unawares. People supped in gaily-lighted cafés and took their substantial meals without thought of the morrow. There were fewer women in the streets and the workmen carried rifles, but the shops were still attractive in their wares. The fear of spies occupied men's thoughts rather than the fear of hunger—a foreign accent was suspicious enough to cause arrest! There were few Englishmen in the capital, but those few ran the risk of being mistaken for Prussians, since the lower classes did not distinguish between foreigners.

Paris was invested on September 19th, 1870, and the citizens had experienced terrible want. In October Wilhelm established his headquarters at Versailles, part of the French Government going to Tours. Gambetta, the new minister, made every effort to secure help for France. He departed from Paris in a balloon, and carrier pigeons were sent in the same way to take news to the provinces and bring back offers of assistance. Strange expedients for food had been proposed already, and all supplies were very dear. Horseflesh was declared to be nutritious, and scientists demonstrated the valuable properties of gelatine. Housewives pored over cookery-books to seek for ways of using what material they had when beef and butter failed. A learned professor taught them how to grow salads and asparagus on the balconies in front of windows. The seed-shops were stormed by enthusiasts who took kindly to this new idea.

Gambetta's ascent in the balloon relieved anxiety for a time, because every Parisian expected that help would come. But soon gas could not be spared to inflate balloons and sturdy messengers were in request who dared brave the Prussian lines. Sheep-dogs were sent out as carriers after several attempts had been frustrated, but the Prussian sentries seized the animals, and pigeons were soon the only means of communication with the provinces.

The Parisians clamoured for the theatres to be opened, though they felt the pangs of hunger now. They retorted readily when there was some speech of Nero fiddling while Rome burned. Their city was not yet on fire, they said, and Napoleon, the Nero of the catastrophe, could not fiddle because he had no ear for music! The Cirque National was opened on October 23rd, though fuel was running short and the cold weather would soon come.

In winter prices rose for food that the fastidious had rejected earlier in the siege. A rat cost a franc, and eggs were sold at 30 francs the dozen. Beef and mutton had disappeared entirely from the stalls, and butter reached the price of fifty francs the demi-kilogramme. The poor suffered horrible privations, and many children died from the effect of bread soaked in wine, for milk was a ridiculous price. Nevertheless, four hundred marriages were celebrated, and Paris did not talk of surrender to their Prussian foes.

Through October and November poultry shops displayed an occasional goose or pigeon, but the sight of a turkey caused a crowd to collect, and everyone envied those who could afford to purchase rabbits even though they paid no less than 50 francs. Soon dogs and cats were rarely seen in Paris, and bear's flesh was sold and eaten with avidity. At Christmas and New Year very few shops displayed the usual gifts, for German toys were not popular at the festive season and the children of the siege talked mournfully of their "New Year's Day without the New Year's gifts."

Shells crashed into houses in January of 1871, an event most startling to Parisians, who had expected a formal summons to surrender before such acts took place. After the first shock of surprise there was no shriek of fear. Capitulation was negotiated on January 26th, not on account of this new danger, but because there was no longer bread for the citizens to buy.

Gambetta resisted to the last, but his dictatorship was ended, and a National Assembly at Bordeaux elected M. Thiers their president. By the treaty of Frankfort, signed in May 1871, France ceded Alsace and Lorraine to Prussia, together with the forts of Metz, Longwy and Thionville. She had also to pay a war indemnity of £200,000,000 sterling. By the exertions of Bismarck, the imperial crown was placed upon the head of Wilhelm I, and the conqueror of France was hailed as Emperor of United Germany in the Great Hall of Mirrors at Versailles by representatives of the leading European states. The German troops were withdrawn from Paris, where civil war raged for some six weeks, the great buildings of the city being burned to the ground.

Europe was satisfied that united Germany should take the place of Imperial France, whose policy had been purely personal and selfish since its first foundation in 1852. The fall of Napoleon III caused little regret at any court, for he had all the unscrupulous ambition of his mighty predecessor, without the genius of the First Napoleon.

Chapter XIX

The Reformer of the East

ITALY had won unity after a gallant struggle, and Greece some fifty years before revolted from the barbarous Turks and became an independent kingdom. The traditions of the past had helped these, since volunteers remembered times when art and beauty had dwelt upon the shores of the tideless Mediterranean. Song and romance haloed the name of Kossuth's race when the patriot rose to free Hungary from the harsh tyranny of Austria. General sympathy with the revolutionary spirit was abroad in 1848, when the tyrant Metternich resigned and acknowledged that the day of absolutism was over.

It was otherwise with the revolting Poles, who dwelt too far from the nations of the West to rouse their passionate sympathies. France promised to help their cause, but failed them in the hour of peril. Poland made a desperate struggle to assert her independence in 1830, when Nicholas the Autocrat was reigning over Russia. The Poles entered Lithuania, which they would have reunited with their ancient kingdom, but were completely defeated, losing Warsaw, their capital, and their Church and language, as well as their own administration.

Under Nicholas I, a ruler devoted to the military power of his Empire, there was little chance of freedom. He had himself no love of the West and the bold reforms

The Reformer of the East

which might bring him enlightened and discontented subjects. He crushed into abject submission all opposed to his authority. The blunt soldier would cling obstinately to the ancient Muscovy of Peter. He shut his eyes to the passing of absolutism in Europe and died, as he had reigned, the protector of the Orthodox Church of Russia, the sworn foe of revolutionaries.

Alexander II succeeded his father while the Crimean war was distracting the East by new problems and new warfare. Christian allies fought for the Infidel, and France and England declared themselves to be on the side of Turkey.

At the famous siege of Sebastopol, a young Russian officer was fighting for promotion. He wrote vivid descriptions of the battle-fields and armies. He wrote satirical verses on the part played by his own country. Count Leo Tolstoy was only a sub-lieutenant who had lived gaily at the University of Kazan and shared most of the views of his own class when he petitioned to be sent to the Crimea. The brave conduct of the private soldiers fighting steadfastly, without thought of reward or fear of death, impressed the Count, with his knowledge of the self-seeking, ambitious nobles. He began to love the peasantry he had seen as dim, remote shadows about his father's estate in the country. There he had learnt not to treat them brutally, after the fashion of most landowners, but it was not till he was exposed to the rough life of the bastion with Alexis, a serf presented to him when he went to the University, that Tolstoy acquired that peculiar affection for the People which was not then characteristic of the Russian.

After the war the young writer found that, if he had not attained any great rank in the army, high honours were awarded him in literature. Turgeniev, the veteran novelist, was ready to welcome him as an equal. The gifted officer was flattered and fêted to his heart's content before a passionate love of truth withdrew him from society.

After the death of Nicholas reaction set in, as was inevitable, and Alexander II was eager to adopt the progress of the West. The German writers began to describe the lives of humble people, and their books were read in other lands. Russia followed with descriptions of life under natural conditions, the silence of the steppes and the solitude of the forest where hunter and trapper followed their pursuits far from society.

Tolstoy set out for Germany in 1857, anxious to study social conditions that he might learn how to raise the hapless serfs of Russia, bound, patient and inarticulate, at the feet of landowners, longing for independence, perhaps, when they suffered any terrible act of injustice, but patient in the better times when there was food and warmth and a master of comparatively unexacting temper.

Tolstoy had already written *Polikoushka*, a peasant story which attracted some attention. He was in love with the words People and Progress, and spoke them continually, trampling upon conventions. A desire to be original had been strong within him when he followed the usual pursuits of Russians of fashion. He delighted in this wandering in unknown tracks where none had preceded him. He was sincere, but he had not yet taken up his life-work.

At Lucerne he was filled with bitterness against the rich visitors at a hotel who refused to give alms to a wandering musician. He took the man to his table and offered wine for his refreshment. The indignation of the other guests made him dwell still more fiercely upon the callousness of those who neglect their poorer neighbours. Yet the quixotic noble was still sumptuous in his dress and spent much time on the sports which had been the pastimes of his boyhood. He nearly lost his life attempting to shoot a she-bear in the forest. The beast drew his face into her mouth and got her teeth in the flesh near the left eye. The intrepid sportsman escaped, but he bore the marks for long afterwards.

In 1861 a new era began in Russia, and a new period in Tolstoy's life, which was henceforward bound up with the history of the country folk. Alexander II issued a decree of emancipation for the serf, and Tolstoy was one of the arbitrators appointed to supervise the distribution of the land, to arrange the taxes and decide conditions of purchase. For each peasant received an allotment of land, subject for sixty years to a special land-tax. In their ignorance, the serfs were likely to sell themselves into new slavery where the proprietors felt disposed to drive hard bargains. Many landlords tried to allot land with no pasture, so that the rearer of cattle had to hire at an exorbitant rate. There had been two ways of holding serfs before—the more primitive method of obliging them to work so many days a week for the master before they could provide for their own wants, and the more enlightened manner of exacting only *obrók*, or yearly tribute. Tolstoy had already allowed his serf to " go on *obrók*," but, according to himself, he did nothing very generous when the new act was passed providing for emancipation.

He defended the freed men as far as possible, however, from the tyranny of other landowners, who began to dislike him very thoroughly. He had won the poor from their distrust by an experiment in education which he tried at his native place of Yasnaya Polyana.

The school opened by Count Tolstoy was a "free" school in every sense of the word, which was then becoming popular. The children paid no fees and were not obliged to attend regularly. They ran in and out as they pleased and had no fear of punishments. It was a firm belief of the master that compulsory learning was quite useless. He taught in the way that the pupils wished to learn, humbly accepting their views on the matter. Vivid narration delighted the eager peasant boys in their rough sheepskins and woollen scarves. They would cry "Go on, go on," when the lesson should have ended. Any who showed weariness were bidden to "go to the little ones." At first, the peasants were afraid of the school, hearing wonderful stories of what happened there. They gained confidence at length, and then the government became suspicious.

Tolstoy had given up his work with a feeling of dissatisfaction and retired to a wild life with the Bashkirs in the steppes, where he hoped to recover bodily health, when news came that the schools had been searched and the teachers arrested. The effect on the ignorant was to make Tolstoy seem a criminal.

Hatred of a government, where such a search could be conducted with impunity, was not much modified by the Emperor's expression of regret for what had happened. The pond on Tolstoy's estate had been dragged, and cupboards and boxes in his own house opened, while the floor of the stables was broken up with crowbars. Even the diary and letters of an intimate character which had been kept secret from the Count's own family were read aloud by gendarmes. In a fit of rage, the reformer wrote of giving up his house and leaving Russia "where one cannot know from moment to moment what awaits one."

The Reformer of the East

In 1862 Tolstoy married Sophia Behrs, the daughter of a Russian physician. He began to write again, feeling less zeal for social work and the need to earn money for his family. The *Cossacks* described the wild pleasures of existence away from civilization, where all joys arise from physical exertion. Tolstoy had known such a life during a sojourn in the Caucasus. It attracted him especially, for he was an admiring follower of Rousseau in the glorification of a return to Nature.

On the estate of Yasnaya there was work to be done, for agricultural labour meant well-cultivated land, and that meant prosperity. A large family was sheltered beneath the roof where simplicity ruled, and yet much comfort was enjoyed. Tolstoy wore the rough garments of a peasant, and delighted in the idea that he was often taken for a peasant though he had once been sorely troubled by his blunt features and lack of physical beauty. Family cares absorbed him, and the books he now gave to the world in constant succession. His name was spoken everywhere, and many visitors disturbed his seclusion. *War and Peace*, a description of Napoleonic times in Russia, found scant favour with Liberals or Conservatives in the East, but it ranked as a great work of fiction. *Anna Karenina* gave descriptions of society in town and country that were unequalled even by Turgeniev, the writer whose friendship with Tolstoy was often broken by fierce quarrels. The reformer's nature suffered nothing artificial. He sneered at formal charity and a pretence of labour. Hearing that Turgeniev's young daughter sat dressed in silks to mend the torn and ragged garments of poverty, as part of her education, he commented with his usual harshness. The comment was not forgiven, and strife separated men who had, nevertheless, a curious attraction for each other. Fet, the Russian poet was, indeed, the only friend in the literary world fortunate enough always to win the great novelist's approbation.

As the sons grew up, the family had to spend part of the year in Moscow that the lads might attend the University. It was necessary to live with the hospitality of Russians of the higher class, and division crept into the household where father and mother had been remarkable for their strong affection. Tolstoy wore the sheepskin of the labourer and the felt cap and boots, and he ate his simple meal of porridge at a table where others dined with less frugality. He had given up the habits of his class when he was fifty and adopted those of the peasantry. In the country he rose early, going out to the fields to work for the widow and orphan who might need his service. He hoped to find the mental ease of the manual labourer by entering on these duties, but his mind was often troubled by religious questions. He was serving God, as he deemed it, after a period of unbelief natural to young men of his station.

He had learnt to make boots and shoes and was proud of his skill as a cobbler. He gave up field sports because they were cruel, and renounced tobacco, the one luxury of Mazzini, because he held it unhealthy and self-indulgent. Money was so evil a thing in his sight that he would not use it and did not carry it with him. "What makes a man good is having but few wants," he said wisely. There were difficulties in the way of getting rid of all his property, for the children of the family could not be entirely despoiled of their inheritance. There were thirteen of them, and they did not all share the great reformer's ideas.

In 1888, Tolstoy eased his mind by an act of formal

renunciation. The Countess was to have charge of the estates in trust for her children. The Count was still to live in the same house, but resolved to bind himself more closely to the people. He had volunteered to assist when the census was taken in 1880 and had seen the homes of poverty near his little village. He had been the champion of the neighbourhood since he defended a young soldier who had been unjustly sentenced. There was always a knot of suppliants under the " poor people's tree," ready to waylay him when he came out of the porch. They asked the impossible sometimes, but he was always kindly.

Love for the serf had been hereditary. Tolstoy's father was a kindly-natured man, and those who brought up the dreamy boy at Yasnaya had insisted on gentle dealings with both men and animals. There was a story which he loved of an orderly, once a serf on the family estate, who had been taken prisoner with his father after the siege of Erfurt. The faithful servant had such love for his master that he had concealed all his money in a boot which he did not remove for several months, though a sore was formed. Such stories tallied with the reformer's own experiences of soldiers' fighting at Sebastopol.

His mind was ever seeking new ways to reach the people. He believed that they would read if there were simple books written to appeal to them. He put his other labours on one side and wrote a series of charming narratives to touch the unlettered and draw them from their passion for *vodka*, or Russian brandy, and their harmful dissipations. *Ivan the Fool* was one of the first of these. The *Power of Darkness* had an enormous popularity. The A B C books and simple versions of the Scriptures did much to dispel sloth of mind in the peasant, but the Government did not look kindly on these efforts. To them the progressive Count was dangerous, though he held apart from those fanatics of the upper classes who had begun to move among the people in the disguise of workers, that they might spread disturbing doctrines.

The police system of Russia involved a severe censorship of literature. Yet only one allusion did Tolstoy make in his *Confessions* to the revolutionary movement which led young men and women to sacrifice their homes and freedom from a belief that the section of society which they represented had no right to prey upon the lower. Religion, he says, had not been to them an inspiration, for, like the majority of the educated class in Russia, they were unbelievers. Different in his service toward God and toward Mankind was the man who had begun life by declaring that happiness came from self-worship. He prayed, as age came upon him, that he might find truth in that humanity which believed very simply as others had believed of old time, but he could not be satisfied by the practises of piety. He was tortured until he built up that religion for himself which placed him apart from his fellows who loved progress.

The days of persecution in the East were as terrible as in the bygone days of western mediæval tortures. For their social aims, men and women were condemned to death or banishment. The dreary wastes of Siberia absorbed lives once bright and beautiful. Known by numbers, not by names, these dragged out a weary existence in the bitter cold of an Arctic winter. "By order of the Tsar" they were flogged, tormented, put in chains, and reduced to the level of animals, bereft of reason. Fast as the spirit of freedom raised its head, it was cowed by absolutism and the powerful machinery of a Government that used the wild Cossacks to overawe the hot theories of defenceless students. Educated men were becoming more common among the peasants, thanks to Tolstoy's guidance. He had shown the way to them and could not repent when they took it, for it is the duty of the reformer to secure a following. Anarchy he had not foreseen, and was troubled by its manifestations. The gentle mind of an old man, resting peacefully in the country, could not penetrate the dark corners of cities where the rebellious gathered together and hatched plots against the tyrant. In spite of Alexander's liberal measures, the Nihilists were not satisfied with a Government so despotic. Many attempts had been made to assassinate him before he was killed by a hand-bomb on March 13th, 1881.

Alexander III abandoned reforms and the discontent increased in Russia, where the plots of conspirators called forth all the atrocities of the spy-system which still existed. Enmity to the Government was further roused in a time of famine, wherein thousands of peasants perished miserably. Tolstoy was active in his attempts to relieve the sick and starving in the year 1891, when the condition of the people was heartrending. He received thanks which were grateful to one very easily discouraged. The peasants turned to him for support quite naturally in their hour of need.

Trouble came upon the aged leader through a sect of the Caucasian provinces who had adopted his new views with ardour. The Doukhobors held all their goods in common and made moral laws for themselves, based on Tolstoy's form of religion. They refused to serve as soldiers, which was said to be a defiance of their governor. The leaders were exiled and some hundreds enrolled in " a disciplinary regiment " as a punishment,

Tolstoy managed to rouse sympathy for them in England, and they were allowed to emigrate instead of suffering persecution. He wrote *Resurrection*, a novel dealing with the terrible life of Russian prisons, to get money for their relief. He was excommunicated formally for attacking the Orthodox Church of Russia in 1901. The sentence caused him to feel yet more bitterly toward the Russian government. He longed to see peace in the eastern land whence tales of cruelty and oppression startled the more humane provinces of Europe. He would fain have stayed the outrages of bomb-throwing which the Nihilist societies perpetrated. He could feel for the unrest of youth, but he knew from his long experience of life that violence would not bring them to the attainment of their objects.

The tragedy of the Moujik-garbed aristocrat, striving for self-perfection and cast down by compromise made necessary by love for others, drew to a close as he neared his eightieth year. He would have given everything, and he had kept something. Worldly possessions had been stripped from his dwelling, with its air of honest kindly comfort. More and more the descendant of Peter the Great's ambitious minister began to feel the need of entire renunciation. It was long since he had known the riotous life of cities, but even the peace of his country retreat was broken by discords since all did not share that longing for utter self-abnegation which possessed the soul of Leo Tolstoy, now troubled by remorse.

In the winter of 1910 the old man left the home where he had lived in domestic security since the first years of his happy marriage. It was severe weather, and his fragile frame was too weak for the long difficult journey he planned in order to reach a place of retreat in the

The Reformer of the East

Caucasus Mountains. He had resolved to spend his last days in complete seclusion, and to give up the intercourse with the world which made too many claims upon him. He died on this last quest for ideal purity, and never reached the abode where he had hoped to end his days. The news of his death at a remote railway station spread through Europe before he actually succumbed to the severity of his exposure to the cold of winter. There was universal sorrow, when Tolstoy passed, among those who reckoned him the greatest of modern reformers.

Chapter XX

The Hero in History

ACROSS the spaces of the centuries flit the figures known as heroes, some not heroic in aspect but great through the very power which has forbidden them to vanish utterly from the scenes of struggle. Poets who wrote immortal lines and philosophers who mocked the baseness of the age which set up shams for worship, reformers with a fierce belief in the cause that men as good as they abhorred to the point of merciless persecution—these rank with the soldier, rank higher than the monarch whose name must be placed upon the roll because his personality was strong to mould events that made the history of his country. High and low, prince or peasant—all knew the throes of struggle with opposing forces, since without effort none have attained to heroism.

Back into the Middle Ages Dante and Savonarola draw us, marvelling at the narrow limits which bound the vision of such free unfettered minds. The little grey town of Tuscany lives chiefly on the fame of the poet and preacher who loved her so passionately though she proved a cruel and ungrateful mother. The Italian state has ceased to assert its independence, and the brawling of party-strife no longer draws the mediator to make peace and, if possible, secure to himself some of the rich treasures of the Florentines whose work was coveted afar. Pictures of wondrous beauty have been defaced and stolen, statuary has crumbled into the dust that lies thick upon the tombs of great men who have fallen. But the words of the *Divine Comedy* will never be forgotten, and the glory of an epic rests always with Italian literature. All the cold and passionless intellect of the Renaissance can be personified in Lorenzo the Magnificent, who encouraged the pagan creeds that the Prior of San Marco yearned to overthrow. Enemies in life, they serve as opposing types of the fifteenth century Italian, one earnest, ardent, filled with zeal for self-sacrifice, the other an epicure, gratifying each whim, yet deserving praise because in every form he encouraged beauty. There is something fine in the magnanimity of the Medicean tyrant when he tried to conciliate the honest monk; there is something infinitely noble in the very weakness of the martyr, whose death disappointed so many of his followers because it proved that he had not miraculous powers.

The charm of Southern cities makes the background for the drama between man and the devil seem dingy in comparison, but even Central Europe has romantic figures in the Reformation times. No sensuous Italian mind could have defied Pope and Emperor so stoutly and changed the religion of many European nations without the world being drenched in blood. Luther is a less gallant champion than William of Orange who fought for toleration and lost life and wealth in the cause, but his words were powerful as weapons to reform the ancient abuses of the Church. He is singularly steadfast among the ranks of men struggling for freedom of the soul, but hardly daring to war against the cramping dogmas of the past.

The soldiers of the Catholic Church have all the glamour of tradition to render them immortal—they are the saints now whose lot was humblest upon earth. The Crusader has clashed through the ages with the noise of sword and armour, attracting the lover of romance, though he performed less doughty deeds than the monk of stern asceticism, whose rule forbade him to break peace. He enjoys glory still as he enjoyed the hour of victories, and the battle that might bring death but could not result in shame. The Brethren of St Dominic and St Francis shrank in life, at least, from the reverence paid to the sacrifice of worldly pleasures. They were marvellously simple, and believed that only some stray picture on their convent walls would remain to tell their story. They judged themselves unworthy to be praised, and their creed of cheerful resignation would have forbidden them to accept the adulation of the hero-worshipper which was lavished in their age upon more brilliant warriors of the Church.

Time has had revenge upon the Grand Monarch and the usurping tyrant, yet their names must be upon the roll of heroes, since they played a mighty part in the events that make history and cannot suffer oblivion though they have ceased to tower above the subjects they despised. Louis XIV's personality needs the mantle of magnificence which fell from France after the predominance of years. Napoleon can be watched in obscurity and exile till the price of countless victories is estimated more truly now than was possible for his contemporaries. His successor has become a mere tinsel figure meddling with strange impunity with the destinies of Europe, and possessing qualities so little heroic that only his audacious visions and his last great failure make the memory of France's last despotic ruler one that must abide with the memory of those other Revolutionaries of 1848.

Mazzini and Garibaldi receive once more the respect that poverty stripped from them when they led a forlorn cause and gave up home and country. Earthly admiration came too late to console them for the ills of exile and the loss of their beloved, but they both knew that a struggle had not been vain which would leave Italy free. Romance forgets these sons of the South and their brief taste of popular glory. Youth looks further back for idols placed on pinnacles of tradition, despising shabby modern garb and loving the blood-stained suit of armour.

Rousseau has risen triumphant above the strife of tongues that would dispute his claims to the heroic because his life was marred and incomplete. He has credit now for a fierce impersonal love of truth and purity. He is a great teacher and a great philosopher, though none ever placed him among the heroic in action or in character. His cynical contemporary, Voltaire, still has some veil of vague obscurity which hides his brilliance from the world apt to reckon him a mere scoffer and destroyer of beliefs. He has more profound faith perhaps than many who took up the sword to defend religion, but he covered his spirit of tolerance with many cloaks of mockery, ashamed to be a hero in conventional trappings, eager to win recognition for his wit rather than immortality for the courage of the convictions he so firmly held.

Not of equal stature are the heroes looming through the curtain Fate drops before each scene of the world's drama when another play begins. There were selfish aims sometimes in the breasts of the patriotic, worldly ambitions in the Reformers, the lust of persecution in the Saints. Yet these great protagonists of history are easy to distinguish among the crowd of actors who have played their parts. Their words grip the attention, their actions are fraught with real significance, and it is they who win applause when the play is at an end.

Index

Aboukir, 175, 177
Aboukir Bay, 174
Acre, 175, 177
Addison, 158
Ajaccio, 168, 171
Albizzi, Rinaldo degli, 31
Albizzi, the, 30, 31
Aldgonde, Sainte, 92
Alençon, Prince, 109
Alexander II, Emperor of Russia, 217, 218, 219, 220, 225
Alexander III, Emperor of Russia, 225
Alexander, Emperor of Russia, 178
Alexander of Parma, 97
Alexandria, 174
Alexis, 137, 138, 144
Alfonso of Naples, 32
Alighieri, Durante, 21
Alma, Battle of, 209
Alps, the, 207
Alsace, Province of, 215
Alva, Duke of, 82, 87, 88, 89, 90, 91, 93
Amelia, Daughter of George I, 148
America, discovery of, 40
Amiens, Treaty of, 176
Amsterdam, 93, 139
Anna Karenina, 221
Angelico, Fra, 31
Angelo, Michael, 127
Angoulême, Duchess of, 180
Anita, wife of Garibaldi, 197
Anjou, 18, 45, 106, 111
Anjou, Duke of, 97, 98
Anna of Saxony, Princess, 80
Anne of Austria, 91, 118, 129

Anthony of Bourbon, 103
Antwerp, 86, 91, 95, 98
Apostolato, Popolare, the, 191
Apraxin, Admiral, 142
Aragon, Prince of, 18
Archangel, 138
Arezzo, 22
Aristotle, 16
Armand Jear. Duplessis, 116, 117
Arouet, Francois Marie (see Voltaire)
Arques, Battlefield, 116
Arrabiati, the, 49
Artois, Count of, 180
Assisi, 14
Athens, Duke of, 30
Auerstädt, Battle of, 178
Augsburg, 56, 61, 71
Augustine, Saint, 53
Augustus, King of Poland, 142, 149
Augustus, William, 149
Austerlitz, Battle of, 178
Austria, 64, 70, 91, 96, 118, 121, 129, 151, 156, 172, 173, 175, 179, 180, 183, 186, 188, 192, 198, 202, 208, 209, 210
Austria, Emperor of, 202
Azov, 139

Balaclava, Battle of, 209
Bassi, Ugo, 193, 198, 204
Barras, 172
Bartholomew, Saint, Massacre of, 92, 107
Bassompierre, 125
Bastile, the, 125, 157, 171
Bavaria, 150
Bavaria, Dukes of, 14
Bayard, Knight, 67, 68
Béarns, 102
Beatrice, 21, 22, 23, 24, 28

Beauharnais, Eugene, 172, 184
Beauharnais, Hortense, 207
Beauharnais, Josephine, 172, 177, 207
"Beggars, The," 84, 85, 86, 90, 92, 94, 95
Beghards, the, 13
Bègue, Lambert Le, 13
Béguines, 13
Behrs, Sophia, 221
Belgium, 211
Bellerophon, the, 182
Berlaymont, 83, 84
Berlin, 145, 160, 178
Berne, 174
Biagrasse, La, 67
Bianchi, the, 24
Bismarck, Herr Otto von, 210, 215
Blücher, 182
Bohemia, 152, 201
Bologna, 20, 26, 42, 69
Bonaparte, Charles, 169
Bora, Catherine von, 60
Bordeaux, 215
Borodino, Battle of, 180
Borsi, Marquis, 41
Botticelli, 38, 39
Boulogne, 178
Bourbon, 102
Bourbon, Constable of, 67, 68
Bourges, Archbishop of, 13
Brabant, Duke of, 86, 98
Brandenburg, Elector of, 145
Brederode, noble, 83, 84
Brienne, 169
Brill, 92
Brussels, 71, 83, 84, 88, 96
Buonaparte, Jerome, 179
Buonaparte, Joseph, 179

233

Buonaparte, Louis, 179
Burgundy, 64, 65

Cairo, 174
Cajetan, Papal Legate, 56
Calais, 73
Calas, 164
Calvin, John, 100, 163
Cambalet, Marquis of, 126
Camicia Rossa, **the**, 197
Camisaders, the, 93
Campanile, the, 32
Cambalet, Madame de, 127
Cane della Scala, 28, 29
Canossa, 14
Caprera, 201
Carbonari, the, 185, 186, 187, 188
Carlyle, 191
Casimir, John, 97
Cateau Cambrésis, 75
Catherine de Medici, 101, 102, 104, 105, 106, 108, 109, 110
Catherine of Aragon, 64, 66
Catherine, Queen, 140, 143
Catholic League, the, 112, 114
Cavalcanti, Guido, 22
Cavour, Count, 199, 200, 201, 202, 205, 206
Cencio, 15
Cerchi, the, 21, 24
Charles Albert, King of Sardinia, 192, 194, 196, 201
Charles I of England, 122, 129
Charles II of England, 133
Charles II of Spain, 132
Charles V, 57, 63, 64, 65, 66, 67, 68, 69, 70, 71, 72, 73, 74, 75, 78, 80, 100
Charles VI of Austria, 150
Charles VII, 67
Charles VII, Emperor, 151
Charles VIII of France, 45, 46, 47

Charles IX, 101, 104, 105, 106, 108, 109
Charles X, 186
Charles XII of Sweden, 140, 142, 145, 149, 152
Charles, Count of Anjou, 18, 45
Chartres, 114
Châtelet, Marquis du, 159, 160
Chevreuse, Madame de, 124
Chièvres, Flemish Councillor, 66
Chillon, Marquis de (see Richelieu), 117
Christ, 10, 38, 54, 58
Christianity, 11
Ciompi, the, 30
Cirey, 159, 160
Civil Code, the, 176
Cloth of Gold, Field of the, 65
Colbert, 130, 135
Coligny, Admiral de, 98, 99, 106, 107, 108
Columbus, Christopher, 64
Commune, the, 166
Compiègne, 208
Concini, 118, 119
Concordat, the, 176
Condé (Enghien), General, 129, 133, 137
Condé, Prince de, 106
Confessions, Tolstoy's, 224
Conrad, 18
Conradin, 18
Constantinople, 12, 32
"Continental System," the, 180
Corneille, 131
Corsica, island, 168, 170, 171
Cosimo dei Medici, 31, 32, 33, 34
Cossacks, the, 221
"Council of Trouble" (Blood), 89, 91
Crimea, the, 200, 209
Cromwell, Protector, 170
Crusades, the, 11

D'Aiguillon (see Madame de Cambalet)
D'Albert of Navarre, 65
Dante Alighieri, 21, 22,
23, 24, 25, 26, 27, 28, 29, 30, 32, 187, 228
Delft, 95, 98
De Luynes, 119, 120
Denis, Madame, 161, 162
Deptford, 139
Desaix, General, 175
Dettingen, Battle of, 151
Devin du Village, Le, play, 165
Diet of Spires, 61
Diet of Worms, 57, 58
Dijon, 101
Directory, the, 173, 174
Divine Comedy, the, 28, 29, 229
Domenico, Fra, 49, 50, 51
Dominic, Saint, 13, 42, 230
Dominicans, 13, 43
Donati, Lucrezia, 34
Donati, the, 21, 23, 24, 26
Don John, 96, 97
Doukhobors, the, 225
Dresden, Treaty of, 152
Dreux, 113
Duc d'Enghien, 129
Duplessis, Armand Jean, 116

Egmont, Count, 79, 80, 81, 85, 87, 88, 89
Egypt, 174, 175, 177
Eisenach, 57
Eisleben, 52, 62
Elba, 180, 181, 182
Elizabeth, Queen of England, 90, 95, 97, 106, 108
Émile, 165
Enghien (Condé) (see Condé, General)
England, 63, 65, 69, 122, 135, 150, 152, 153, 157, 168, 172, 175, 176, 180, 182, 209, 211
Epérnon, General, 119
Erasmus, 55, 60
Erfurt, 52, 56, 223
Eric, Duke of Brunswick, 58
Eugénie, Empress, 208, 211, 212
Evelyn, John, 139

Fæsulæ, 20
Farinata degli Uberti, 19

Index

Fénélon, Priest, 134
Ferdinand, 63
Ferdinand I, 184, 192, 200, 205
Ferdinand II, Emperor, 126
Ferdinand of Bohemia, 120
Ferney, 162
Ferrara, 41
Fet, Poet, 222
Flanders, 81, 135
Fleury, General, 202
Florence, 19, 20, 21, 22, 23, 25, 26, 27, 29, 30, 31, 32, 34, 35, 36, 37, 38, 39, 40, 44, 46, 47, 48, 49, 51
Flushing, 92
France, 17, 25, 27, 45, 63, 65, 66, 67, 69, 70, 74, 75, 85, 92, 95, 103, 109, 120, 121, 122, 123, 125, 126, 129, 130, 131, 135, 150, 152, 153, 168, 172, 175, 176, 201, 203, 207, 216
Francis I of France, 57, 63, 64, 65, 67, 68, 113
Francis II of Austria, 184, 202, 205
Francis Joseph II, Emperor, 202, 205
Francis, Saint, 13, 230
Franciscans, 13
Frankfort, 54, 61, 151, 180
Frankfort, Treaty of, 215
Frate, the, 27
Frederick II, 15, 17, 18
Frederick II, of Brandenburg and Hohenzollern, 147, 148, 149, 150, 151, 152, 153, 154, 156, 160, 161, 178
Frederick, Elector of Saxony, 53, 55, 64
Frederick, Elector Palatine, 120
Frederick, Prince of Wales, 148
Frederick William I, 145, 146, 147, 148, 154, 156
Fronde, La, 129
Frondeurs, the, 129

Galitzin, 137, 138
Gambetta, 213, 215
Gaston, brother of Louis XIII, 124
Garibaldi, 193, 196, 197, 198, 199, 201, 203, 204, 205, 206, 207, 210, 230
Gay, 158
Gemma, 23
Geneva, 162, 164, 165, 166, 190
Genoa, 12, 168, 186, 189
George I of England, 148
George II of England, 151
Germany, 61, 62, 69, 70, 74, 85, 100, 154, 218
Ghent, Pacification of, 96
Ghibellines, 14, 16, 19, 22, 25
Giotto, 32
Giuliano, 38, 39
Gordon, Patrick, 140
Granvelle, Cardinal, 78, 79, 81
Greece, 175
Grenoble, 181
Grisi, 191
Guelfs, the, 14, 15, 16, 19, 22
Guise, Duke of, 103, 107
Guise, Henry of, 102, 108, 109, 112

Haarlem, 93, 94
Hamburg, 61
Henry II of France, 71, 75, 109
Henry III of France, 110, 112, 114
Henry, IV of Germany, 14
Henry IV of France, 114, 116
Henry VI, 15
Henry VIII, 59, 63, 64, 65, 70
Henry of Anjou, 106, 111
Henry d'Albret, 113
Henry de Bourbon, 105
Henry of Guise, 102, 108, 111
Henry of Luxembourg, Emperor, 27, 28
Henry of Navarre, 97, 104, 106, 108, 109, 110, 111, 112, 113, 115

Henry, Prince of Bourbon, 102, 104
Henry of Valois, 112
Hohenlinden, Battle of, 175
Hohenstaufen, House of, 15, 17
Hohenzollern, House of, 210
Holland, 83, 85, 93, 95, 96, 98, 133, 179
Holy Land, 12
Holy Wars, 12
Homer, 28
Hoorn, Admiral, 85, 86, 89
Hubertsburg, 153
Huguenots (Confederates), 101, 102, 108, 118, 120, 123
Hungary, 65

Imola, Tower of, 37
India, 153, 174
"Indulgences," 54
Inferno, the, 26, 27, 29
Inkerman, Battle of, 209
Inquisition, the, 70, 76, 82, 83
Isabella, 63
Isabella of Portugal, 67
Italy, 12, 15, 17, 20, 27, 42, 45, 64, 67, 69, 122, 127, 173, 174, 175, 183, 184, 185, 186, 188, 189, 191, 192, 200, 201, 202, 203, 206, 207, 210
Ivan, half-brother of Peter the Great, 137
Ivan the Fool, 223
Ivry, Battlefield, 116

Jaffa, 175
Jansenists, the, 163
Jarnac, Battle of, 104
Je l'ai vu, play, 157
Jena, 59, 178
Jerusalem, 12, 15
Jesuits, the, 163
Joanna, daughter of Ferdinand and Isabella, 63
John of Austria, 96

Katte, Lieutenant von, 149
Kléber, 177

Kneller, Sir Godfrey, 139
Knox, John, 100

La Barre, 164
Ladies' Peace, The, 68
Lambert Le Bègue, 13
Landgrave of Hesse, 70
"League of the Compromise," 82, 83
Lebœuf, Marshal, 211
Lefort, 138
Legion of Honour, the, 176
Leibnitz, 159
Leipzig, Battle of, 180
Leo X, Pope, 54, 55
Leonora, wife of Concini, 118, 119
Leopold, Prince, 210, 211
Lesser Brothers, 14
Leszczynski, Stanislaus, 142
Lettres anglaises, 158
Leuthen, 152
Leyden, 94
Lille, Battle of, 135
Lisle, Rouget de, 176
Livonia, 140
Livy, 32
Locke, 158
Lombardy, 43, 68, 184, 202, 203
Longwy, Fortress of, 215
Lorenzo, Church of San, 32
Lorenzo the Magnificent, 33, 34, 35, 36, 37, 38-41, 43, 229
Lorraine, Province of, 215
Louis XI, 65
Louis XIII, 118, 119, 122, 124, 127
Louis XIV, 129, 130, 131, 132, 133, 134, 135, 137, 154, 230
Louis XVI, 165, 176, 180, 208
Louis XVIII, 180
Louis, Count of Nassau, 82, 90, 92, 93, 94, 96
Louis de Bourbon, 103, 104
Louis Philippe, King, 86, 207, 208
Louis, Saint, of France, 113
Louvain, 89

Louvre, the, 104, 117, 130
Low Countries, the, 63, 74, 75, 78, 80, 82, 87, 89, 90, 93
Lowe, Sir Hudson, 182
Lucerne, 218
Luçon, Bishop of, 117, 118, 119, 120
Ludovico, 37
Lulli, 132
Lunéville, Treaty of, 176
Luther, Johnny, 60
Luther, Martin, 52, 53, 54, 55, 56, 57, 58, 59, 60, 61, 62, 69, 70, 100, 229
Luxemburg, 211
Luxemburg, Henry of, 27
Lyons, 17, 181

Madrid, 67
Madrid, Treaty of, 68
Magenta, Battle of, 202
Maggiore, Lake, 201
Magyars, 10
Mahomet, 9
Maintenon, Madame de, 133, 134, 136
Malines, 93
Malta, 69, 174, 175
Mameli, poet, 193
Manfred, 18
Manin, President of Venice, 198
Mantua, Duke of, 122
Marbœuf, 169
Marches, the, 206
Marco, San, 39, 41, 43, 48, 49, 50, 229
Marengo, Battle of, 175
Margaret of Parma, 78, 80, 83, 84, 86, 88, 89
Margaret of Valois, 104, 105, 106, 108
Margrave of Baireuth, 149
Maria Theresa, 132, 150, 151, 152, 153, 156, 172
Marie Antoinette, 166, 172, 208
Marie de Medici, 119, 123, 125, 126, 127
Marie Louise, 177, 179, 180, 184
Marillac, Marshal, 125

Marino, San, 184
Marlborough, Duke of, 135
Marly, 131
Marmont, 173
Marsala, 204
Marseillaise, the, 176
Marseilles, 188
Martino, San, 21, 202
Mary, Queen of Scots, 101
Mary, Princess, 66
Matthias, Archduke, 96
Maurice, Duke of Saxony, 70, 71, 80
Maximilian, Emperor, 20
Mayenne, 113
Mazarin, 129, 131, 132
Mazarins, the, 129, 130
Mazeppa, Hetman, 142
Mazzini, Guiseppe, 185, 186, 187, 188, 189, 190, 191, 192, 193, 196, 199, 201, 222, 231
Medici, Cosimo dei, 31, 32, 33, 34
Medici, Lorenzo dei, 38, 39, 40, 41, 43, 48
Medici, Piero, dei 44, 45, 47
Medici, the, 30, 32, 34, 35, 37, 38, 45, 66, 109
Menshikof, 140
Mentana, Battle of, 210
Metternich, Prince, 184, 185
Metz, 212, 215
Mexico, 210
Middelburg, 92
Milan, 20, 35, 36, 37, 64, 65, 66, 67, 174, 192, 202
Milan, Duchess of, 35, 37
Milan, Duke of, 35, 36
Miloslavski, Mary, 137
Miloslavski, Sophia, 137, 138, 143
Mirandola, Pico della, 42, 43
Modena, 184
Molière, 131, 162
Moltke, General von, 211, 212
Molwitz, Battle of, 151
Mons, 93, 97
Monsieur, Peace of, 109

Index

Montebello, Battle of, 201
Monte Video, 197
Montigny, son of Hoorn, 91, 92
Montpensier, Duchess of, 111
Moreau, General, 175
Moscow, 137, 141, 180, 222
Muhlberg, 70
Murat, General, 184

Namur, 96
Nantes, Edict of, 114, 133
Naples, 16, 18, 32, 36, 39, 45, 63, 65, 66, 184, 191, 200
Napoleon Buonaparte, 168, 169, 170, 171, 172, 173, 174, 175, 176, 177, 178, 179, 180, 181, 182, 183, 188, 189, 196, 230
Napoleon, Louis, 193, 201, 207, 208
Napoleon III, 201, 202, 203, 207, 208, 209, 210, 211, 212, 213, 215
Narva, 140
Naryshkin, Nathalie, 137
Nassau, 82
Navarre, 97, 102, 103, 104, 105, 108, 109, 110, 112, 113, 115, 116
Navarre, d'Albert of, 65
Navarre, Princesse de, 159
Nelson, 174, 178
Neri, the, 24
Netherlands, the, 66, 70, 71, 74, 75, 77, 78, 82, 83, 86, 87, 88, 90, 91, 94, 95, 97, 98, 133
Neva, river, 141, 142
New Learning, 63
Newton, 158, 159
New World, 64
Nice, 203
Nicholas I, Emperor of Russia, 216, 218
Niemen, 178
Nihilists, the, 225
Notre Dame, Cathedral of, 118, 129
Nouvelle Héloïse, La, play, 165

Novara, Battle of, 196, 200
Nuremburg, 61

Œpide, tragedy, 157
Orange, Prince of (see William)
Orleans, Duke of, 186
Orsini, Clarice, 34

Palermo, 16, 204, 205
Paoli, 168, 169
Papacy, the, 14, 15, 18, 52, 56, 66, 70
Paradiso, the, 28
Paris, 27, 59, 101, 105, 107, 112, 113, 114, 119, 157, 158, 162, 167, 171, 181, 186, 208, 212, 213
Paris, the Congress of, 200
Parma, Duchess of, 79, 85
Parma, Duke of, 113
Pauline, sister of Napoleon, 199
Pavia, 67
Pazzi, Carro dei, 37
Pazzi, banking-house of, 37, 38, 39, 40
Pazzi Conspiracy, 36
Pazzi, Francesco dei, 37
Peter, Prince of Aragon, 18
Petersburg, Saint, 141, 142, 144, 145
Peter the Great, 137, 138, 139, 140, 141, 142, 143, 144, 145, 226
Philip, Archduke of Austria, 64
Philip II, Emperor of Spain, 71, 75, 76, 77, 81, 84, 87, 88, 89, 92, 93, 97, 98, 105, 113, 118
Philip IV of Spain, 122
Philip, King of France, 25
"Piagnoni" (Snivellers), 47, 49, 50
Piedmont, 184, 189, 193, 199, 200
Pilo, Rosalino, 204, 205
Pisa, 12
Pisa, Archbishop of, 30, 39
Pisa, Lord of, 28

Pistoia, 24
Pitt, William, 178
Pius IV, 41
Pius VII, 184
Plasencia, city of, 72
Plato, 32
Plautus, 53
Poitou, 117
Poland, 150, 216
Poland, King of, 141, 142
Polikoushka, 218
Poltava, Battle of, 142
Pomerania, province, 152
Pompadour, Madame de, 158, 166
Pont Neuf, 117
Pope Alexander VI, 45 48
Pope Boniface, 25
Pope Clement VII, 68
Pope Gregory VII, 14
Pope Gregory IX, 15, 16
Pope Innocent IV, 16, 43, 44
Pope Julius, 68
Pope Leo X, 54, 66
Pope Sixtus IV, 36, 42
Pope, the, 14, 16, 37, 41, 47, 48, 53, 62, 64, 69, 173, 208
Portinari, the, 21
Portinari, Beatrice, 22
Portugal, 67, 105, 133, 179
Portugal, King of, 105
Potsdam, 160, 161
Potsdam Guards, 145, 146
Poussin, 127
Power of Darkness, the 223
"Pragmatic Sanction" the, 150
Prague, 152
Preaching Brothers, 14
Pressburg, 151
Prior, 158
Protestants, 61, 78, 86, 92, 93, 109, 114, 122
Prussia, 145, 148, 150, 152, 153, 156, 160, 180, 209, 210, 211, 215
Puglia, Francesco da, 49, 50

Purgatorio, the, 28
Pyrenees, Treaty of, 130

Quatre, Henri, 113

Racine, 131
Radetsky, Field-Marshal, 195
Rambouillet, Julie de, 127
Ramolino, 189
Ramolino, Letitia, 168
Ravaillac, 115
Ravenna, 29
Requesens, Don Luis, 94, 95
Resurrection, Tolstoy's, 226
Revival of Letters, 55
Revolution, French, 155, 170
Rheims, 114
Rheinsburg, Castle of, 149
Rhodes, 69
Riario, 37, 38
Richelieu, Cardinal, 115, 116, 117, 118, 119, 120, 121, 122, 123, 124, 125, 126, 127, 129
Rochelle, La, 109, 121
Rocroy, Battle of, 129
Rohan, Chevalier, 157
Rohan, Duke of, 122
Roman Emperor, the Holy, 64
Roman Empire, 68
Rome, 13, 15, 20, 24, 25, 38, 47, 54, 55, 56, 61, 101, 117, 121, 195, 196, 197, 198, 204, 207, 210
Roon, General von, 212
Rossbach, Battle of, 152
Rotondo, Monte, Battle of, 210
Rouen, 103
Rousseau, Jean-Jacques, 164, 165, 166, 167, 230
Ruel, 127
Ruffini, Jacopo, 189, 191
Russia, 139, 141, 142, 152, 156, 172, 179, 180, 200, 209, 217, 219, 224
Ryssel, 79
Ryswick, Peace of, 135

Sadowa, Battle of, 209, 210
Saint Augustine, Order of, 53
Saint-Cyr, Convent of, 133
Saint Dominic, 13, 42, 230
Saint Francis, 13, 230
Salemi, city of, 204
Salviati, Archbishop, 38
Sansoni, Cardinal Raffaelle, 38
San Yuste, Monastery of, 71, 72
Sardinia, 184, 198, 199, 201, 204, 205
Sardinia, King of, 184, 194, 196, 204, 205
Savonarola, Girolamo, 45, 46, 47, 48, 49, 50, 51, 52, 57, 228
Savoy, 69, 122, 190, 203
Savoy, Duchy of, 184, 198, 206
Saxony, 59, 70, 80, 150, 152, 179
Saxony, Elector of, 53, 58, 61, 70, 87
Sayes Court, 139
Scala, Cane della, 28
Scarron, Poet, 133
Sebastopol, Siege of, 217, 223
Sedan, Battle of, 212
Segovia, Castle of, 91
Seine, river, 9
Selim, 65
Sepulchre, the Holy, 11
Servetus, 100
Sforza, Galeazzo, 35, 37
Sicily, 63, 184, 191, 204, 205, 206
Silent, William the (see William)
Silesia, 150, 151, 152, 153
Simone de Bardi, 22
Social Contract, the, 165
Solferino, Battle of, 202
Soliman the Magnificent, 69
Sorbonne, the, 101, 112
Spain, 63, 64, 67, 70, 76, 78, 81, 86, 87, 90, 91, 97, 105, 118, 122, 126, 130, 133, 150, 179, 210

Spain, King of, 86, 104
Speyer, Diet of, 61
Staël, Madame de, 180
States-General, the, 81, 95, 96
Staupnitz, 53
St Bartholomew, Massacre of, 92, 107
St Helena, 182
St Jerome, brothers of, 72
St John, Knights of, 69
St Peter's, 16, 53, 54
Streltsy, the, 138, 139
Sully, 114
Susa, Pass of, 122
Swabia, 14, 18
Swarte, John de, 79
Sweden, 141, 142
Swift, Jonathan, 157
Switzerland, 190
Syria, 175

Tetzel, 54, 55
Thiers, Monsieur, 215
Thionville, Fortress of, 215
Third Estate, the, 158
Thirty Years' War, 126
Tilsit, Treaty of, 178, 180
Titelmann, Peter, 78
Titian, 72
Toledo, Duke of Alva, 88
Toleration, Edicts of, 111
Tolstoy, Countess, 223
Tolstoy, Count Leo, 217, 218, 219, 220, 221, 222, 223, 224, 225, 226, 227
Torriano, 73
Toulon, 172
Tours, 213
Trafalgar, Battle of, 178
Trianon, village, 166
"Troubles, Council of," 89
Tuileries, the, 104, 180, 181, 210
Turenne, General 133, 137
Turgeniev, novelist, 217, 221
Turin, 206
Turkey, 140, 142, 200, 208, 217
Tuscany, 19, 184, 192
Tyrol, the, 201

Index

Uguccione, Lord of Pisa, 28
Umbria, 206
United States, 198
Urbino, Duke of, 37

Valladolid, 76
Valois, Henry of, 112
Vassy, 103
Vatican, the, 117
Venetia, 202
Venice, 12, 20, 36, 184, 198, 203, 205, 206, 210
Vergil, 27, 28, 53
Verona, 28
Versailles, 130, 131, 132, 134, 154, 159, 213, 215
Victor Emmanuel II, 196, 198, 202, 203, 204, 205, 206, 207
Victor Emmanuel, King, 184
Vienna, 183, 185, 192, 198
Voltaire, 136, 156, 157, 159, 160, 161, 162, 163, 164, 165, 166, 167, 231
Volterra, town of, 36, 38, 40
Volturno, Battle of, 206

Waiblingen (Ghibellines), 14
Walcheren, 92, 95
War and Peace, 221
Warsaw, 216
Waterloo, Battle of, 182
Weaving Brothers, 13
Weimar, 57
Welf, 14
Wellesley, Sir Arthur, 179, 182
Wellington, Duke of (see Wellesley)
Westphalia, 179
Wilhelm I, Emperor, 210, 211, 212, 213, 215
Wilhelmina, 147, 148, 149

Wilhelmus van Nassouwen, 92
William III of England, 135, 139
William, Prince of Orange, 75, 79, 80, 81, 83, 85, 86, 87, 89, 90, 92, 93, 94, 95, 96, 97, 98, 99, 103, 108, 229
William the Stadtholder, 135
Wittenburg, 53, 55, 56, 58, 59, 62
Wolsey, Cardinal, 65
Worms, 57, 58, 61, 69
Wörth, Battle of, 212

Yasnaya Polyana, 219, 221, 223

Zaandem, 139
Zealand, 93, 95, 96, 98
Zierickzee, 95
Zorndorf, Battle of, 152
Zutphen, 93

APR 2 6 2003